"*Imagine a funnel. Conversion Rate Optimization is like widening the bottom so more of your visitors become paying advocates. Jon does a superb job explaining the applied science of e-commerce optimization. This is one of those practical studies that I wish I'd published at 2PM.inc! I soaked it up.*"

—WEB SMITH, FOUNDER OF 2PM.INC.

"*In this book, Jon teaches you how to give your customers the 'Kim Kardashian on the red carpet' treatment, which is a recipe for success in any market conditions. Having this book when I started out would've saved me tons of time and helped me avoid hard lessons learned through trial and error. I'll be handing a copy of this book to the teams I work with, and I hope you spend time with it, too.*"

—NIK SHARMA, FOUNDER OF SHARMA BRANDS

"You can't open your browser without seeing a best practices listicle or Twitter thread about 'guaranteed wins.' This book, thankfully, is not more of that. Opting in to Optimization is unlike anything else out there. Jon has a unique gift for sharing what truly works—based on his real-world experience helping multi-million dollar brands scale—while telling stories that help new concepts feel like familiar friends. Trust me, you want to read this book before your competitors do."

—VAL GEISLER, CUSTOMER EVANGELIST AT KLAVIYO

"I've been banging the drum on customer retention for years, and this book shines a light on one of my favorite retention strategies—providing an outstanding customer experience from day one. Jon has created the perfect resource for e-commerce leaders who want to crush their revenue goals using customer-centric design. Buy it. Read it. Thank me later."

—KRISTEN LAFRANCE, SHOPIFY

"They say that you need to dress for the job you want. Well, leaders at early-stage e-commerce brands should pay close attention to the concepts in this book because they are the foundational elements required to compete with the larger, more established brands in e-commerce."

—BEN JABBAWY, PRIVY

"Jon effectively demystifies and maps out approaches that have taken years to understand and adopt across e-commerce teams for any size company. If you were going to get the best e-commerce product leaders in a room and have them break down the years of experience they have had, it would be this book."

—ALAN WIZEMANN, GOOP, TARGET, LULULEMON, DOLLAR SHAVE CLUB

"This book doesn't pull any punches! Jon shows you how applying 'best practices' is the path to mediocrity and teaches you how to create a custom optimization strategy that will help your brand rise above competitors. My perspective on e-commerce growth has been changed forever, and I recommend that other founders add this to their bookshelf right away."

—JASON WONG, WONGHAUS VENTURES AND DOE LASHES

"This is a must-read for any founder or marketer in the e-commerce space. Jon & The Good have helped me remove myself from the day-to-day grind and start thinking again like a customer. We're investing heavily in customer experience in order to increase customer lifetime value and improve education on our niche sport. With just a few small tweaks, we've already seen incredible progress in our most important metrics."

—CHRIS MEADE, CROSSNET

"I've built my entire business on helping brands earn more revenue with email marketing, but driving traffic is only half the battle. I can't think of anyone more qualified than Jon to teach you how to design high-converting purchasing experiences and maximize the value of every visit."

—CHASE DIMOND, BOUNDLESS LABS

"I've watched Jon consistently uncover conversion opportunities for close to one hundred brands over the years. One even implemented his suggestions on the spot—the night before Black Friday—and had record sales. He's my first call for all things e-commerce CRO."

—CASEY ARMSTRONG, SHIPBOB

"Conversion rate optimization is like CX; there's no silver bullet. It takes continuous listening, iterating, and testing to get even close to perfect. Jon has a deep understanding of what to do, and even more so, what not to do, to make your website do the work!"

—ELI WEISS, OLIPOP

"I've known and talked optimization with Jon for more than five years. And what he and his team have taught me about their approach—over countless, patient hours—is packed into this book. So think of it as a cheat code. If you need further convincing, though, consider this line from one of the pages inside: 'by the time you hear about best practices, they're quickly approaching their "best if used by" date.' You won't find them here. Instead, you'll find the keys to understanding what's best for your business. So while Jon is great company and a worthwhile friend, the book may be a quicker way to success with regard to improving your business."

—LEO STRUPCZEWSKI, REPEAT

"Very few people understand consumer behavior better than Jon and his team at The Good. That's why I jumped at the opportunity to learn from someone who knows how to convert browsers into buyers. I'm convinced these are the fundamental frameworks needed to get ahead (or stay ahead) as e-commerce continues to get more competitive going forward. This is a must-have for any e-commerce founder's bookshelf."

—HUGH THOMAS, UGLY DRINKS

OPTING IN TO OPTIMIZATION

R. Jon MacDonald

OPTING IN TO OPTIMIZATION

How Successful E-commerce Brands
Convert More Customers, Increase Profits,
and Create Raving Fans

HOUNDSTOOTH PRESS

OPTING IN TO OPTIMIZATION

How Successful E-commerce Brands Convert More Customers, Increase Profits, and Create Raving Fans

ISBN   978-1-5445-2496-2 *Hardcover*

978-1-5445-2495-5 *Paperback*

978-1-5445-2497-9 *Ebook*

978-1-5445-2540-2 *Audiobook*

CONTENTS

*Here's to removing all the
bad online experiences until
only the good remain.*

ACKNOWLEDGMENTS

This book would not have been possible without the many wonderful, brilliant team members who have been part of The Good's mission over the last decade-plus to remove all the bad online experiences until only the good ones remain. Because of you, the internet is a better place.

A special thank-you to Natalie Thomas and James Sowers, who both contributed their time, effort, and thought leadership to help this book take shape.

Especially worthy of recognition is Laura Bosco, who made major contributions to getting this book written and whose patience, guidance, and editing along the way made it all possible.

FOREWORD

BY NIK SHARMA
CEO, SHARMA BRANDS
FORBES 30 UNDER 30
INVESTOR AND ADVISOR TO JUDY, CARAWAY
HOME, HINT, HAUS, AND MANY OTHER
FAST-GROWING E-COMMERCE BRANDS

There's been writing on the wall for a while now about a shift in e-commerce.

Customer acquisition costs are rising, competition has increased in most markets, and it's easier than ever to create and control a decentralized workforce (not to mention company). Tack on global challenges, rising unemployment, and a shifting economy, and you find yourself here, right in the middle of e-commerce 3.0.

The companies that succeed in e-commerce 3.0 won't be built and run the same way the companies that succeeded in 2.0 were. Too much has changed. The tried-and-true "formulas" that used to work won't. To survive in this new landscape, brands will need to shift the way they think about building, launching, and operating. It's not enough to have just another moisturizer that competes with the other 3,500 moisturizers on the market, even if your superficial label does look nice on Target's shelf.

The brands least likely to succeed will miss this.

They'll spend six figures on branding, forklift money into Facebook, or take out two-page glossy adverts in *Forbes*. They'll follow old playbooks, formulas, and "best practices," assuming what worked for Native or Warby Parker will work for them, too.

And they'll be passed by the brands most likely to succeed, who take a different path.

The brands most likely to succeed (like JUDY, Haus, Caraway, and others I've worked with over recent years) will be hyperfocused on their customers. They'll also be hyperfocused on profitability, stretching their dollars, running meaningful tests, and reducing risks at every turn.

Smart founders are tuning in to this. Which is why one of

the most common questions I get these days is, "What's the number one thing I can do to better my revenue?"

My answer: increase the on-site conversion rate of your store. Simply put, in this day and age, you can't afford not to have a conversion-optimized website.

Don't get me wrong, "increase conversions" is easy enough to say, but it's hard to do well. That's partially because conversion rate optimization is widely misunderstood.

See, increasing conversion rates doesn't mean adding neat graphics to a landing page, spending seven figures on paid social, or using fancier adjectives to describe your products' cool features. All that stuff misses the point, misses the customer.

Increasing conversion rates means (as I've often said) treating your customer like they're Kim Kardashian on the red carpet. They're the star; you're the assistant. And you need to have everything ready for your star to read, understand, and act on. You have to know what they want, when they want it, and why they even want it to begin with. And then you have to do something that looks like magic—you have to meet their needs before they even vocalize them.

Think of it this way. You don't expect Kim to navigate around the red carpet, get hangry, find a takeout place during a bathroom break, and order a salad from her phone in a stall (this is how assistants get fired, by the way). No, you already have the salad ready to go, with the exact toppings that meet her diet and nutrition needs, before she knows she's hungry. And then you deliver it at the perfect break-in-the-action moment.

Sure, your customers may not want a plant-based salad with five cherry tomatoes to chow down on between press comments. Maybe they want Taco Bell, or an afternoon burst of energy, or to feel prepared for an unexpected emergency. But whatever it is they want, they want it quickly so they can get back to whatever it was they were doing. They want to be treated like they're Kim, and you're helping them live a more flawless life. To put that in e-commerce terms, it's your job to understand site visitors and then make their conversion fast and easy.

This book teaches you the principles of how to do all that well. How to Kim Kardashian your customer, roll out the red carpet, increase your conversion rates, and set your brand up for compounding success in the 3.0 e-commerce setting.

It teaches offensive conversion rate optimization principles like *always be testing*, incentivizing without slashing margins, and really getting to know your customer. And it teaches defensive plays, too, such as creating rock-solid brand equity and providing the kind of customer experience that digs a deep moat around your brand. (And trust me, a deep moat is one of your biggest advantages in e-commerce 3.0!)

What's more, this book teaches you how to apply those offensive and defensive principles with empathy. Jon and his team at The Good know e-commerce brands are built by humans and for humans. (Bots aren't buying flavored water; real humans who want to stay on top of their diets are.) And so there's a "humanness" to this book, a rooted belief that compassion for site visitors matters much more than silver bullets, quick conversions, or sharp-edged short-cuts, which tend to do more harm than good anyway.

Finally, this book will save you time. Jon demystifies conversion rate optimization and dispels misunderstandings that continue to trip up even experienced founders (Is there a good conversion rate? Are big tests better? What about redesigns?). And he openly shares what I—and most founders—have had to learn by trial and error, years of messing stuff up, or other grueling, sweat-and-blood methods. Frankly, I wish I had this book when I started out. It would've saved me a good deal of time and a good many U-turns.

I've always been a fan of giving away my best secrets, and that's what Jon does here. For anyone willing to listen, he cracks open the strategic playbook he's built from years of driving higher conversions for brands like Xerox, Swiss Gear, Easton, Adidas, Converse, and many, many others. Jon is on a mission to remove all the bad online experiences until only the good remain. This book is your invitation to join that big mission and your guide to fulfilling it within your brand.

I'll be handing a copy of this book to my teams and the teams I invest in, and I hope you spend time with it, too.

After all, every e-commerce business could use more conversions, and the world could certainly use more good experiences!

INTRODUCTION

Phil Jackson has more NBA championship rings than any other coach—thirteen, to be exact. Two he earned as a player with the New York Knicks. The other eleven he earned as a coach—six as head coach of the Chicago Bulls and then five more with the Los Angeles Lakers.

To get those legendary eleven, he did something no one else did at the time.

Head coaches work high-stakes jobs in the cutthroat, competitive environments of NBA pro basketball and American capitalism. In the eighties and nineties (Jackson's era), most head coaches took a militaristic approach. They fumed, shouted, flaunted power moves, and shoved players into rigid systems. No other approach, it seemed, could pave the way to championship rings.

Until Phil Jackson showed up. And the only thing more surprising than his approach was the fact that it worked.

Most coaches taught players to focus on titles; Jackson encouraged players to focus on each other. Most coaches set up strict, uniform regimens for players; Jackson crafted a unique approach for each athlete's strengths and weaknesses. (He treated dazzling Michael Jordan differently than hotheaded Dennis Rodman—and coaxed both enormous egos into operating as team players.) Most coaches visualized championship rings as symbols of power and status; Jackson taught his team they represented a circle of team compassion.

To use language from his book *Eleven Rings*, Phil Jackson focused on "the soul of success." That's what made him different from other coaches. He cared about titles, yes. But to him, rings and winning were the results of a healthy team soul, not the causes of it. Get the principles right, and the rest follows.

You may never have set foot on a basketball court. But you, too, are in a highly competitive world where a "win at all costs" mindset dominates. In e-commerce, the stakes are high—and getting higher as the industry accelerates and has a growing valuation in trillions of dollars.

I've little doubt if you've picked up this book, you have an e-commerce site, and you've already invested a considerable amount of time, energy, and money into driving traffic to that site. I suspect you've worked very hard on generating wins like subscriptions, revenue, or more customers, too.

I also suspect something keeps you up at night.

Maybe traffic isn't converting like you think it should, or the tactics you're using aren't working the way they did for a rising direct-to-consumer darling. At any rate, something isn't adding up. You're short on rings and wins.

If this sounds familiar, you're not alone. As the Founder and CEO of The Good, a conversion rate optimization firm, I encounter this scenario every week. I've spent over twelve years helping the world's largest brands like Nike, Xerox, Adobe, *The Economist* (and hundreds of smaller, yet well-known brands) successfully optimize their sites.

You're not Nike any more than you're Phil Jackson, but here's the good news: with the right approach, you can earn the results many of the brands I've worked with have seen. Results like increased conversions leading to an average increased revenue of over 100 percent.

You can make that happen. But not, perhaps, the way you'd expect.

You won't get there with a bag of in-favor hacks, a guide

to the latest Shopify app promising huge conversion gains, or a twenty-seven-tips roundup claiming changing button colors will double your online revenue (spoiler: it won't).

Rather, you need something that goes much deeper—something that, like Phil Jackson's effective and revolutionary coaching approach, goes right to the soul of success. In e-commerce terms, you need a collection of conversion principles. Principles so proven over time that for brands of every size, they're more like laws.

That's what you're holding. The immutable conversion laws in this book outline everything you need to know about the approach, practice, and mindsets that generate more conversions and revenue for brands of every size. Even better, you don't need decades of experience, an unusual amount of skill, the best players in the industry, or millions of dollars in salary to apply them.

You just need a willingness to know who's coming to your site,[1] a curiosity to dig into what they're experiencing, and the humility to make their experience better.

The laws in this book—backed by a decade-plus of conversion rate optimization learnings—will take you from there.

---

[1] The content of this book is applicable to all lead-generation sites. For the sake of simplicity, we have chosen to use e-commerce terminology throughout. Apart from not having a checkout process, the basic proposition of a lead-generation site is essentially the same as that of an e-commerce site: provide value by helping people do the things they want to do.

GOAL OF THIS BOOK

My goal is for you to walk away from this book with new approaches to optimizing your site for conversions and a new way to think about how conversion optimization is synonymous with a good user experience.

At its core, conversion rate optimization is about removing as much friction from a website experience as possible, so nothing inhibits a consumer from researching and purchasing a product. This benefits the customer AND you—at the end of the day, you both want a conversion: the brand for sustainable revenue, the consumer to solve the pain or need that brought them to your brand in the first place.

The laws of conversion optimization contained within this book are the truths that have rung true time and again, for over a decade, for brands of every size.

Avoid them at the peril of your brand.

WHO IS THE GOOD?

The Good (thegood.com) is a conversion rate optimization firm. We help brands to convert more of their existing website visitors into buyers.

We've spent years developing, testing, and improving methods to increase conversion rates and grow revenues online. There are plenty of references to "we" throughout this book, and wherever they are, I'm referring to The Good.

WHOM THIS BOOK IS FOR

This book outlines a path to successful e-commerce site design and optimization. The strategies and tactics discussed are equally applicable to all lead-generation sites. For the sake of simplicity, we have chosen to use e-commerce terminology throughout. Apart from not having a checkout process, the basic proposition of a lead-generation site is essentially the same as that of an e-commerce site: provide value by helping people do the things they want to do. Whether you run an e-commerce site or a lead-generation site, this book will help you grow your revenues by better understanding and serving your prospects and customers.

CHAPTER 1

LAW: BEST PRACTICES ARE FOR BEGINNERS

Big idea: Best practices are good training wheels for a new brand, but they quickly cap how much a mature brand can convert. True conversion rate optimization demands a more tailored approach.

Most companies that walk through the doors of my agency, The Good,[2] want the fruits of data-driven marketing but aren't sure how to pick them. Sometimes, they're not even sure they're in the right forest. That's why they come to us.

We're experts in conversion rate optimization—understanding the clicks and movements of website visitors and using

---

2   You can learn more about The Good at thegood.com.

that data to convert more visitors into buyers. We peer into the data forest and find the trees, the low-hanging fruit, and the long-term opportunities for better experiences and revenue.

Our approach, part art and mostly science, works. For over a decade, we've generated incredible results for some of the largest online brands, including Adobe, Nike, Xerox, Verizon, Intel, and others. In recent years, brands that work with us have seen an average increase of revenue of over 100 percent.

But conversion rate optimization doesn't just "happen," and it certainly doesn't work the way most people think it does.

It's not dumping out a bag of tricks, gimmicks, hacks, or shady manipulation on a site. It's not copying what the big brands or rising stars are doing either. At its core, *it's not even about your brand*. It's about valuing your customers, getting to know them, and removing all the bad experiences until only the good ones remain.

And here's the first thing you need to know: "best practices," while good-intentioned, are toxic for a growing team.

DIAGNOSE BEFORE PRESCRIBING

Think of the last time you visited the doctor with an injury or pain. Imagine if instead of receiving a physical or detailed personal history, the doctor shook your hand and gave you a prescription. "What's this?" you'd ask.

"Oh, it's something that works for most people," she'd say on her way to see other patients.

Even if she wrote you a prescription for strong Tylenol, you'd have every right to be wary of that recommendation. After all, the doctor doesn't even know where your pain is, let alone what caused it! Yet, this is the way most folks approach conversion rate optimization—with a "works for most people" prescription.

The intention—optimizing your website so it converts more visitors—is good. True conversion rate optimization can deliver amazing results for an e-commerce brand. Some of the results our team at The Good has generated include a 132 percent year-over-year revenue increase for Swiss Gear, a 659 percent (that's not a typo) mobile revenue growth increase for Easton, and an 86.7 percent increase in return visitor conversions for Xerox. And that's just a sampling of the kind of ROI our clients see. Conversion rate optimization works, and pursuing it is a worthwhile investment.

But you don't get those results by checking off a standard list of best practices (filling a generic prescription) for your site before you know where it hurts. In conversion rate optimization, you need to diagnose before you prescribe.

WHY BEST PRACTICES ARE SO POPULAR ANYHOW

Before we wade into diagnostics, though, let's look at why best practices are even a thing. Why are managers and store owners drawn to them to begin with?

It'd be easy to call best practices a "lazy approach" and dismiss folks who use them as "people simply looking for a silver bullet." Although Americans certainly do love a quick fix, most store owners and e-commerce managers are far from lazy—starting your own online business is a notable feat, and keeping that business alive is an enormous undertaking! No, the reasons we're drawn to best practices run deeper than "I don't feel like trying," and understanding those reasons is useful for moving beyond them.

One of the main things best practices do is give us a sense of order and control. Running a business or department can feel like wading against a river of entropy; it seems most systems, teams, and websites default to chaos without constant guidance. Best practices look like strong guidance, like a trustworthy paddle that'll keep you moving upstream against all that chaos. We see them and say, "I can make this change and see that improvement." And this gives us a sense of control.

They're also widely accepted. When a large number of people (especially official-looking people) say, "This is good," we nod our heads. Psychologists call this social conformity. They've found we're more likely to pay taxes when we know others do,[3] we're more likely to give to charity when it's the norm,[4] and we'll even decrease how much energy we use if we're told we're using more than our neighbors.[5] No one wants to be an outcast. Best practices help us fit in.

On top of that, best practices are very accessible ("conversion rate optimization best practices" returns *fifteen million results* on Google). And in addition to building the reputation of thought leaders, quite a few of these practices do help brands.

For example, using high-contrast colors on your website is a user experience best practice. It ensures folks can read the words on your page without wanting to tear their eyes out. It also ensures anyone with color blindness, acute vision loss, or cognitive impairment can navigate your site. Usability and inclusivity are good things.

What's more, I've published plenty of best practices myself—standard ways to optimize checkout (show progress), improve search (have autocomplete), and level up product detail pages (high-quality images). I publish

---

3   Stephen Coleman, "The Minnesota Income Tax Compliance Experiment: Replication of the Social Norms Experiment," SSRN (2007), https://papers.ssrn.com/sol3/papers.cfm?abstract_id=1393292.

4   Sarah Smith, Frank Windmeijer, and Edmond Wright, "Peer Effects in Charitable Giving: Evidence from the (Running) Field," *The Economic Journal* 125, no. 585 (2013): 1053-71, https://doi.org/10.1111/ecoj.12114.

5   Hunt Allcott, "Social Norms and Energy," *Journal of Public Economics* 95, no. 9-10 (2011): 1082-95, https://www.sciencedirect.com/science/article/abs/pii/S0047272711000478?via%3Dihub.

those because best practices like these are sturdy training wheels—which is why I say they're for beginners. If you're just figuring out how to pedal your e-commerce store, they can give you a stable (and if you're shrewd about what you adopt, effective) starting point.

There's nothing at all wrong with being a beginner—that's where we all start. The trouble is, most brands keep those training wheels on for far too long.

"THE ROAD TO MEDIOCRITY IS PAVED WITH BEST PRACTICES"

Many wineries in Bordeaux, France improve wine quality with best practices from winemaking consultants. For example, a process called micro-oxygenation means vintners (wine merchants) can store wine for shorter periods and buyers can drink it at a younger age. The downside is, this process makes Bordeaux wines taste similar, minimizing their differences and the vintners' ability to compete. After fifteen years of analyzing business and winemaking, Jérôme Barthélemy, professor of strategy and management at ESSEC Business School in Paris, concluded, "Adopting a best practice is a great way to achieve average results. Not only that: Adopting a best practice that is wrong for your company can destroy value."[6]

---

6   Jérôme Barthélemy, "Why Best Practices Often Fall Short," *MIT Sloan Management Review*, February 27, 2018, https://sloanreview.mit.edu/article/why-best-practices-often-fall-short/.

This is as true for e-commerce as it is for wine. Although best practices can give you stability in your toddler days, they hinder your ability to perform and compete as you grow. They don't make you the best; they make you the average of everyone else applying them. That's because best practices fail to point you toward the right audience, at the right time, in the right way.

RIGHT AUDIENCE: BEST PRACTICES AREN'T TAILORED TO YOUR CUSTOMERS

A direct-to-consumer athletic apparel brand hired a new e-commerce manager with the expectation this hip fireball would improve their website's conversion rate. The new hire had plenty of e-commerce experience and seemed like a perfect fit for the role. They made lots of so-called best practice changes—colloquial language on the home page, animated pop-ups to collect email addresses, revamped product names like Amirite, and a big focus on TikTok.

Soon after, website traffic and sales fell off dramatically. The new e-commerce manager was smart and funny and injected a sense of youthful personality into the website experience, but they missed an important fact: the company's core customers were middle-aged consumers, not twentysomething college students. It's not that twentysomethings are a poor or nonexistent customer base—they're perfect for some brands and products. It's that twentysomethings weren't *the right fit for this brand*. The new manager missed the nuance.

Ultimately, the website refresh failed because the customer experience was tailored to appeal to someone else's audience. Even though the company adhered to a few conversion rate optimization best practices, the results were far from satisfactory because the changes didn't align with the customer.

This is something I hear about often, and you don't have to look far to find it. Take brand collaborations, a best practice that especially took off in 2020. So much so, Retail Brew reported, "When historians look back on 2020, they'll be astounded by the tidal wave of logo collages retailers released." But as the year proved, simply merging [brand] with [trendy name] doesn't guarantee success.

Take Cole Haan and Slack's footwear collaboration. In theory, this was a good idea. The colorful, casual sneaker was supposed to celebrate working from home, something nearly all of us did for most of 2020. It was also supposed to tap into the twelve million professionals using Slack. However, it didn't do either of those things well. Why? Folks who use Slack aren't the same as a Slack community, meaning the audience wasn't nearly as captive as, say, Justin Bieber's fan base. (Bieber, by the way, sent Croc stocks soaring by

13 percent when he hinted at a footwear collab.[7]) On top of this, the sneakers featured little more than the Slack logo and a splash of color at a $120 price point. Reviews were brutal, and Haan only managed to sell out after slashing prices 50 percent.

LOCATION, LOCATION, LOCATION

Another audience-related issue? Best practices are geographic. Think of tea in the continental United States. The best way to brew tea in Georgia is with a cup or more of white sugar. If you order iced tea in a Georgia restaurant, it's going to come as sweet as the pies on the dessert menu. But ask for tea in a northern or western restaurant and you'll need to hunt down Splenda yourself. Similarly, best practices for a high-performing US-based website aren't going to perform the same in the rest of the world.

On the now-retired podcast *Let's Fix Things*, designers Guus Baggermans and Joe Fletcher talked about working with a client in Asia. For the assignment, they compared the differences between American and Japanese websites. To American eyes, the Japanese websites looked complicated, cluttered, and clunky. Frankly, they looked like they were stuck in the 1990s—way behind on the

7   Janet Freund and Josh Fineman, "Justin Bieber's Instagram Photo Sends Crocs Shares Soaring," Bloomberg, October 1, 2020, https://www.bloomberg.com/news/articles/2020-10-01/justin-bieber-s-instagram-photo-sends-crocs-shares-soaring.

whole minimalist design trend. But it turns out the complicated Japanese designs didn't reflect ignorance; they reflected the audience. If the website didn't look complicated, Japanese customers would interpret it as unimportant and poorly functioning.[8] American best practices ≠ Japanese best practices.

Researchers have reached similar conclusions. Pamela Hinds, professor of management science and engineering at Stanford, has contributed to several studies that look at applying best practices across cultures. She concludes, "Best practices are optimized for a particular place and time and don't necessarily transfer well between cultures."[9] What works instead? Focusing on the *intent* (vs. tactics) of a best practice, experimenting with adaptations, and working with a cultural liaison.

If you want to make impactful improvements to the usability of your site, you need to research and understand what your specific customers want versus applying what "everyone" supposedly wants. The more personalized your website experience is to your target audience, the better the results. Don't cater to the herd and walk the wide road of mediocrity.[10] Cater to your customers.

---

8   Episode 31: "Diversity Stops Designers from Ruining Things," *Let's Fix Things* (2017).

9   Pamela Hinds, "Research: Why Best Practices Don't Translate across Cultures," *Harvard Business Review*, June 27, 2016, https://hbr.org/2016/06/research-why-best-practices-dont-translate-across-cultures.

10 Credit to Austin Knight for the turn of phrase, "The road to mediocrity is paved with best practices." https://www.invisionapp.com/inside-design/mediocrity-best-practices/.

Right Time: Best Practices Are Tethered to the Past
(Your Business Is Not)

The second big issue with best practices is they're tethered to the past. They're based on previous trends, dated surveys, or a thought-leader tweet that went viral some time ago. In fact, by the time you hear about best practices, they're quickly approaching their "best if used by" date.

Here's a fun example. In 1712, the English government taxed newspapers according to how many pages they printed. So newspapers went big. They adopted what's called the broadsheet size so they could print more news on fewer pages. Now, this tax was abolished in 1855, but printers continued the broadsheet "best practice" even though it was more expensive and rather unwieldy for readers. When a publisher called the *Independent* decided this was more dated practice than best practice and ditched the broadsheet for a smaller tabloid size in 2004, they received a strong boost in circulation. (*The Independent* added about five thousand readers after the switch.)[11] In 2018, *The Guardian* and *The Observer* also opted for tabloid. (However, by that time, tabloid had arguably passed its best by date as well, since most readers were defaulting to online!)

Successful e-commerce brands aren't the ones looking backward to see what the "big guys" did to get where they

---

11   Claire Cozens, "Readers Switch to Tabloid Independent," *The Guardian*, December 5, 2003,
      https://www.theguardian.com/media/2003/dec/05/circulationfigures.pressandpublishing.

are today or what's been the norm for the past decade. For one, they know what worked for someone else yesterday isn't guaranteed to work for them today. Besides, that's what everyone else is doing! Louis Grenier of *Everyone Hates Marketers* points out best practices aren't only geared toward the herd; they're *applied by the herd*. "Most of your competitors read the same books, go to the same conferences, and follow the same 'influencers' on Twitter," Grenier cautions. "Chances are: they have also implemented this 'best practice.' You and your competitors are only playing catch-up while other companies are busy understanding their customers and testing new experiments that will be recognized as 'best practices' in a few years."[12]

Above-average businesses—the ones converting their target customers in droves—are learning in real time from every click and movement of their current website visitors.

Right Way: Best Practices Hinder Testing and Learning

The third major best practice issue is this: even when best practices contain a good idea, they teach growing brands to apply it the wrong way. Top-result blog posts often lead with a remarkable revenue increase that resulted from implementing a single tactic on their website—such as removing a navigation sidebar to boost conversions 100 percent or

---

12   More from Grenier at https://www.hotjar.com/blog/death-by-best-practices/.

changing button colors to green—but provide little to no context on how or why the tactic worked for them. As a result, these reads teach store owners to apply a box of tricks or cash in on a universal prescription "because we did, and it worked."

This mindset launches store owners into a toxic cycle. It kickstarts what positioning expert April Dunford calls the cycle of marketing meh.[13] In the "meh" cycle, marketers pick a fashionable tactic (e.g., podcasts, TikTok, content marketing) because it's what everyone else is "wearing." They implement it for their business, see mediocre or mixed results, and move on to the next fashionable tactic ("what else is everyone doing?"). The result is marketing that's "meh" at best.

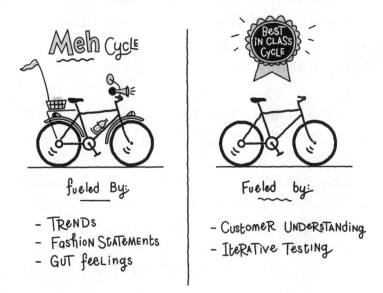

13   Dunford shared this cycle on LinkedIn back in 2014: https://www.slideshare.net/
     aprildunford/markerting-planning-for-startups/6-The_Cycle_of_Marketing_
     MehMarketingFashionAssessmentChooseTacticsExecuteTacticsMeasureResultsDrop.

Applying trendy conversion rate optimization best practices amount to a parallel cycle of conversion meh. You try on whichever tactics popular leaders recommend but find those tactics don't look as good on you as it did on them. Maybe it fits okay on the shoulders, but it's just off everywhere else. So you try on the next thing, and the next thing, and the next. The result? Your site converts "meh" at best.

In both versions of this cycle, you pick a tactic out of the air (or off top Google results for "how to improve conversion rate optimization") and apply the tactic "because they said so" or "because they're doing it," not because "it solves a specific problem for our customers." The result, besides meh conversions and marketing, is you learn surface-level information (and even that at a glacial pace). You're not testing much beyond whether a tactic works, so you don't learn much beyond whether that tactic works.

Put another way, you learn a good deal about correlation and almost nothing about causation. You know whether using Facebook Messenger is correlated with higher revenue or whether free shipping is correlated with a higher number of orders. But (and this is a big problem) you've likely learned nothing about why any of those things are correlated. You don't know *why* those tactics performed the way they did and whether they'll perform that way in the future—this wasn't what you were testing. You were testing whether the tactic looked good on you.

CORRELATION AND CAUSATION AS A
FUNDAMENTAL BEST PRACTICE ISSUE

To take a step back for a moment, the whole correlation versus causation thing is a fundamental problem with best practices as a whole. Many best practices come into prominence for no better reason than a successful company did something interesting. This can lead to some pretty outlandish best practices.

An MIT article recounts a popular creativity myth that Pixar's *bathroom location* (of all things!) is the root of Pixar's renowned creativity.[14] The logic goes that centrally located bathrooms forced employees from different departments to bump into each other. These serendipitous encounters spurred creativity and contributed to Pixar's brilliant storytelling. (Steve Jobs oversaw the architectural plan for the Pixar building and insisted they put the only bathrooms in the atrium, the original idea being that this would force cartoonists and computer geeks into the same space; he compromised on this later.[15]) It's a fun story to tell, and centrally located bathrooms may indeed be correlated with creative teams. But analysts give Pixar's peer culture, which has a big emphasis on candid feedback, the causal credit for creativity, not the bathrooms.

---

14   Barthélemy, "Why Best Practices Often Fall Short."

15   Jonah Lehrer, "Steve Jobs: 'Technology Alone Is Not Enough,'" *The New Yorker*, October 7, 2011, https://www.newyorker.com/news/news-desk/steve-jobs-technology-alone-is-not-enough.

Meh inputs (trends, generalizations) lead to meh outputs. A better cycle starts with better inputs.

THE ROAD TO BEST-IN-CLASS IS PAVED WITH BEST INPUTS, NOT BEST PRACTICES

To summarize so far: applying best practices is like wearing someone else's broken-in shoes. They may look Insta-worthy, and you might be able to walk around in them a little. But they're tailored to someone else's feet; if you keep wearing them, they'll create blisters and calluses that make walking (forget running) very painful.

If you want to outrun the average brands, you need to ditch the kicks other leaders have worn in the past and find a custom fit. To find your conversion rate optimization "custom fit," you need two quality inputs: customer understanding (via non-creepy data collection) and iterative testing.

Customer Understanding

It's borderline impossible to see your site through customers' eyes. You're simply too close to your business and store to experience what new-to-file customers experience—unless you gather data and talk with them. From Google Analytics reports that tell you *what* is happening to customer interviews that illuminate *why* you're seeing certain numbers, there are many ways to uncover your customers' perspective. Collecting that information helps you identify what's tripping them up, where they're left hanging, and how you can improve their journey overall.

Iterative Testing

Once you've studied user interactions on your site and figured out which experiences you definitely need to improve, you can test changes. At The Good, this usually looks like testing a series of small improvements and learning from those results. Over time, these iterative tests compound: the more I know about customers' needs, the easier it is to brainstorm new test concepts in the future.

Why not go bigger, test bigger, move faster? Let's say you read a blog post detailing five tactics to implement on your home page. These tactics are "guaranteed" to improve your conversion rate. After applying all five of the tactics to your website, you notice your conversion rate gradually increases over the next several months. The problem is, you're not sure which tactic provided the positive lift in conversions. So even though something did improve your home page experience, you don't know what, and you won't be able to replicate that success on other pages of your site.

That's why I start small and isolate each modification. It's how I identify which one provides better results for a brand's unique customer base. Rather than five or ten or twenty potential improvements at one time, my team creates a separate A/B test for each and isolates the impact each unique variable has. With this approach, we can be certain the changes you eventually apply to other areas of your website will have a positive impact.

CALORIE-CUTTING TEST APPROACHES AND A WORD OF CAUTION

Here's some basic weight-loss math: more calories burned + fewer calories consumed = smaller weight. As a result, many popular weight-loss programs and apps track calories to help users monitor their weight. This is well-intentioned but fraught with problems. For starters, most people don't know what a calorie IS, besides a number on a nutrition label. Nor do they know their unique calorie needs per day, which is influenced by a whole host of factors. On top of that, you can't draw a straight line from "has fewer calories" to "better for you." A half cup of Cheerios has about seventy calories; an apple has around ninety-five. The apple provides more satisfaction and nutrients for my body than the Cheerios. Yet, counting calories often ignores this nuance. The means are justified, so to speak, so long as the end result is fewer calories.

Teams who simply "test to win" or test to see a number move are prone to the same pitfalls of calorie counting. Quite often, I encounter e-commerce teams that don't care to understand why a specific change to their website caused an uptick in conversions, so long as it did. If a test proves to increase sales, they want to implement the change to their live site as quickly as possible and move on to the next test, regardless of whether the change is healthy for their brand and suited to their customers' needs. It's this mindset that perpetuates the reliance on best practices to grow an e-commerce business.

Yes, an effective conversion rate optimization program will positively influence crucial numbers. But if you're just counting calories (upticks or downticks in conversions), you're not improving the overall health of your brand and customer experience, which means you could do more harm than good long term. Most brands who take the calorie-cutting approach aren't able to maintain sustained progress (let alone an optimization program) because they don't value the big picture. They're quickly disappointed and their overall experience suffers.

To Truly Improve Your Conversion Rate, Start Thinking like a Chef

When popular writer Tim Urban analyzed Elon Musk on the *Wait but Why* blog, he came up with an analogy for the two ways folks operate: the cook versus the chef.[16] A cook is someone who follows recipes (in life as well as in the kitchen). Their starting point is something that already exists—a recipe or conventional wisdom. They do things "because the recipe says so." A chef, on the other hand, is someone who works with raw ingredients to invent a recipe. They look at what's on hand, hypothesize what could be, and taste test until they get to a good outcome.

Chefs often look like magicians or stowaways from the future (see Elon Musk and Steve Jobs). But that's because whereas the cooks rely on conventional wisdom (which is largely based on what was possible years ago), chefs live in the day-to-day data and possibilities. Urban elaborates, "By ignoring conventional wisdom in favor of simply looking at the present for what it really is and staying up-to-date with the facts of the world as they change in real-time...the chef can act on information the rest of us haven't been given permission to act on yet."

In e-commerce conversion rate optimization, cooks follow best practices (recipes). Among the other things we've listed

---

16   Tim Urban, "The Cook and the Chef: Musk's Secret Sauce," *Wait but Why* (blog), November 6, 2015, https://waitbutwhy.com/2015/11/the-cook-and-the-chef-musks-secret-sauce.html.

in this chapter, this means there's a ceiling on how good they can be. They're bound by the recipe. Chefs gather up raw ingredients (customer data), taste test (experiment), and refine until they've made something amazing. There's no ceiling on the improvements they can make—and they see the kind of 100 or even 600+ percent gains I listed at the beginning of this chapter.

So if you're a growing brand, ditch the conventional wisdom training wheels (when you've long since outgrown those!), and look at what your customers are doing or saying. Run tests to solve problems, and pay attention to what each test tells you. Then compound that learning with every consecutive test you run. This is what the most successful e-commerce teams do. After all, true conversion rate optimization isn't a growth hack; it's an iterative process based on customers, testing, and compound learning.

CHAPTER 2

LAW: THE SCIENTIFIC METHOD, NOT SILVER BULLETS

Big idea: Conversion rate optimization isn't a "one and done" guessing game; it's a scientific process based on iteration.

The book (and film) *Moneyball* tells the true story of how the second poorest team in baseball, the Oakland Athletics, won more regular season games than all but one of their twenty-nine competitors. They became one of the most successful franchises in MLB, and they did it with a payroll less than a third of the richest team—a meager $40 million compared to the New York Yankees' $126 million.[17] It was

17   Michael Lewis, *Moneyball: The Art of Winning an Unfair Game* (New York: Norton, 2003).

unprecedented. And it smashed the prevailing rule in base-ball that the teams with the most money always win. How did they pull off this incredible winning streak?

They did it by rethinking baseball. Traditionally, baseball teams evaluated players on a few key metrics—batting average, home runs, RBIs, and so on—and a lot of gut assessment. Literally. The film pokes fun at player reviews such as "passes the eye-candy test," while the book notes scouts' language around players' bodies sounded more like sports car talk than recruiting.

These unscientific evaluation tactics only "worked" for the richest teams who had piles of cash to throw at flashy players. The Oakland A's, with their bottom-of-the-barrel payroll, didn't have that financial luxury, so they needed to find another way. And they did. When they stepped back and looked at the game (in what the book calls "a system-atic scientific investigation of the sport"), they determined wins = getting players on base. So instead of pursuing big hitters who cost half their payroll, they went after players who could get on base, even if the players' methods were non-sexy, such as walks and getting hit by pitches.

They went after meaningful stats instead of pretty faces. This scientific approach worked. The Oakland A's started winning like crazy and kept winning like crazy. Their former general manager (and now EVP) is a living legend because of it. The lesson? Scientific thinking and repeated small achievements (like getting on base) can lead to big results over time.

So what does this story have to do with conversion rates in e-commerce? Well, most brands are stuck in the "old" approach to conversion rate optimization. They think of conversion rate optimization in terms of silver bullets and a "guess and test" approach. They throw a lot of money at pretty players (big redesigns), make gut decisions about improvements ("it's a nice-looking carousel"), and expect both approaches to work.

The only problem is, they don't. Not reliably and not in ways that sustainably improve revenue. Meanwhile, the brands doing something different are the ones pulling ahead and redefining the conversion rate optimization game.

THREE BIG MISCONCEPTIONS ABOUT CONVERSION RATE OPTIMIZATION

Most misconceptions around conversion rate optimization boil down to this: there's a one-and-done way to approach it. Usually, this misunderstanding wears one of three outfits: (1) there's a single "good" conversion rate (or benchmark), (2) a redesign will solve conversion problems, or (3) a big test will deliver all the answers. Here's the problem with each of those.

MISCONCEPTION #1: THERE'S ONE GOOD CONVERSION RATE

"What is a good conversion rate for our e-commerce website?" If there's a list of the top three questions e-commerce VPs ask conversion optimization specialists, that one has to be in first place. When managers ask this, they're typically seeking affirmation of two things:

- First, that they're doing as good or better than their competitors.
- Second, that their conversion rate is performing well.

I understand this. To the first point, it's normal to want to know how you stack up. (We all do this from a young age and well into adulthood.) But really, competitor information won't do anything to improve your own website's conversion rate (see Chapter 9, "Your Competition Is a Distraction," for a laundry list of reasons why). To the second point, no manager wants to spend money on qualified traffic, only to see those visitors leave without some kind of conversion.

The tricky thing is, there's no *one* good conversion rate. We've been asked "What's a good rate?" a thousand times, and our answer has stayed consistent for well over a decade: a good conversion rate is one that is always improving.

A WORD ON BENCHMARKS

A twin misconception here is "industry benchmarks will tell me how we're doing." Benchmarking tells you where your website stands compared to industry-wide averages, and it's a practice we discourage e-commerce businesses from participating in.

First, these averages are faulty. Most brands don't share their true conversion rate. Those that do rarely know how to accurately calculate it, use bad data to do it, and/or use totally different methods to get their final numbers. (We see this all the time when we get "inside" a client's data.) On top of these variables, you've no way to verify whatever rate a company claims. To do so, you'd need access to the company's analytics and reporting, which you won't get.

Even if you get past those hurdles, lumping together like brands for a shared benchmark rarely makes sense. For example, we worked with three eyewear companies at one point in The Good's history. One catered to heavy computer users, another to older adults and stylish readers, and the third to sports enthusiasts. They were all three "eyewear companies," but they had totally different audiences, advertising strategies, channel mix, and seasonality. Yes, they all sold glasses, but comparing their conversion rates would've been like comparing apples to pineapples to papaya—it wouldn't have made sense or helped any of them.

Finally, looking at benchmarks usually has one of two outcomes, neither of which help brands improve their contextual rate:

- **Outcome #1:** You're higher than the industry average, and you feel on top of the world. In this case, most managers will stop investing in optimizing for conversions (they feel it's "good enough") despite how much opportunity is still there. The result is that they leave a lot of revenue on the table.
- **Outcome #2:** You're below the industry average. In this case, managers feel terrible and way behind. This often means they focus on the competition *even more*. (Again, see Chapter 9, "Your Competition Is a Distraction," for why racing the competitor only hurts you.) The result is that they rely on the competition instead of what their own customers and data tell them.

Your most important competitor is yourself. That's why the best conversion rate is one that's always improving.

MISCONCEPTION #2: A REDESIGN WILL TAKE CARE OF OUR CONVERSION ISSUES

If you've been in marketing for much time, you've experienced this cycle: a website frustrates users, traffic stops converting into revenue, and someone starts a redesign.

The problem is, this is a bit like burning down an apartment building when you stop selling units. A redesign torches the building to the ground and starts again on the ashes. You wind up with shinier, trendier units, but there's no guarantee families in the area will want the style or layout you've chosen (even if *you* like it). In fact, there's no guarantee you've solved the original problem at all.

The other option is a slower, more measured approach—a scientific approach. You remodel room by room. You experiment with revamping one unit and gather feedback about what appliances, color schemes, and type of windows your buyers want. Then you take what you learn and apply that to the next unit—and the next, and the next—until you've remodeled every unit in the building.

In both cases, you wind up renovating the building. But in the first approach, you make a lot of guesses. In the second approach, you run small experiments, gather data, and learn as you go. You rebuild around what your buyers want and are guaranteed to move more units because of it.

But our customers often want to know, does the second approach cost more? In our experience, no. However, you should be prepared to take the original lump-sum budget you were going to invest in a redesign and spread it out over a longer period of time while you iterate.

To summarize, redesigns look like a "fast fix," but they don't fix all that much. Compared to improving your conversion rate incrementally, big redesigns are usually

- more disruptive to teams, clients, and customers;
- more expensive to carry out; and
- based on C-suite or founder preferences, not customer-centric data (meaning you get a site that serves executives instead of the customer).

As we pointed out in our first book *Stop Marketing, Start Selling,* through constant iteration, you can turn a poor website into gold and avoid the expensive and often futile cycle of redesigning your entire site every few years. A redesign won't magically lift your revenues; a scientific approach to optimizations will.

MISCONCEPTION #3: BIG TESTS ARE BETTER TESTS

E-commerce brands often think the bigger the test, the better the result. They want to optimize conversions with complex, site-wide experiments that alter multiple website elements in a single A/B test. The logic? The bigger the test, the quicker you can change conversions, and the higher ROI will soar.

This logic sets up a false dichotomy: either you test big and win big, or you test small and win small. Yet, this isn't at all the case.

The size of the test isn't proportional to the size of the results. We've changed one word and improved conversions by 200 percent; we've run giant tests that improve conversions very little. In fact, we have a one to ten rating system for the tests we run. One is a small test you can run immediately, whereas ten is a full-page-redesign kind of test that will take days or weeks to build. When we looked at our data, we discovered level-ten tests weren't more fruitful than small, compounding tests.

On top of that, running a series of small tests early on in an engagement will almost always have a bigger impact than a single big test (that may or may not produce positive results). This is, in part, because big tests exhaust valuable development time, which in turn slows down the velocity at which you're able to launch new tests.

Industry benchmarks, redesigns, big tests, like the old baseball approach of buying flashy big-hitters, signing up for these *can* create a short-term boost in ticket sales (e.g., you redesign, and more folks come to the site to check it out), but that boost won't last long. And then, worse, brand teams are right back where they started but with less budget than they started with. There's a better, more scientific way to approach conversion rates. And like the Oakland A's established, this approach can lead to a long string of wins.

THE BETTER, RIGHT WAY TO APPROACH
CONVERSION RATE OPTIMIZATION

Amazon is perhaps one of the biggest advocates of improving conversions through the scientific method. They're also one of the most successful; Amazon takes a whopping 38.7 percent of e-commerce sales per year.[18] Amazon Founder Jeff Bezos attributes this to experimentation. He said, "Our success at Amazon is a function of how many experiments we do per year, per month, per week, per day."[19] And Bezos experiments relentlessly. In 2011, he ran around 546 experiments per year. By 2013, his teams were running 1,976.[20]

It's no exaggeration to say the growth Amazon has experienced in the last decade is a product of continuous experimentation and improvement. They rely on small bets, incremental improvements, and compounding growth. They're the pinnacle of "easy to buy from" because they've spent the better part of two decades gradually perfecting the customer experience of their website.

This is what we preach at The Good, too: iteration unlocks

---

18   eMarketer Editors, "Target Cracks Top 10 US Ecommerce Ranking," Insider Intelligence, February 28, 2020, https://www.emarketer.com/content/target-cracks-top-10-us-ecommerce-ranking.

19   Ben Clarke, "Why These Tech Companies Keep Running Thousands of Failed Experiments," *Fast Company*, September 21, 2016, https://www.fastcompany.com/3063846/why-these-tech-companies-keep-running-thousands-of-failed.

20   Bezos cites these numbers in a shareowner letter. https://www.sec.gov/Archives/edgar/data/1018724/000119312514137753/d702518dex991.htm.

the long-term benefits of conversion rate optimization because bettering the customers' experience is an ongoing process—one that requires experimentation to get meaningful results. And although there's plenty of nuance to creating a good conversion rate optimization process, the overall framework is one that's useful for any brand to know: set contextual baselines, do exploratory testing, and make continuous improvements.

CONTEXTUAL BASELINES

When you run conversion optimization tests, you'll want to know whether they improve the customer's experience. But if you don't use benchmarks to measure that, what do you use? A baseline specific to your brand and customers. Regardless of where your conversion rate initially sits, this practice helps you sidestep all the pitfalls of benchmarking, and it provides the best results for businesses in the long term. It keeps you focused on incremental improvements to your baseline every month, quarter, and year. It also keeps you focused on your most important competitor—yourself.

EXPLORATORY TESTING

From there, a successful optimization program starts with exploratory testing. This means figuring out how users interact with the site—not to mention who they are—and pinpointing key friction points in the customer journey.

(Refresher: friction is any part of your site or experience where folks stumble—confusing navigation, technology issues, etc.) If you can remove harmful friction, you'll provide a better experience.

At its core, exploratory testing is gathering data on how customers interact with your site, analyzing it, making hypotheses, and running small tests. This works because understanding the ins and outs of individual user interactions opens up a clear path for designing bigger tests later on. What you learn in an initial round of A/B testing lays the foundation for what you focus on throughout the course of the optimization program, and so on, and so on. This is how you get continuous, compounding improvement.

CONTINUOUS IMPROVEMENT

You can always optimize a website further, no matter how satisfied your customers are or how great your conversion rate may be. A great example of this is the online vacation rental website Airbnb. Like a majority of hotel and vacation rental websites, Airbnb relies on their search bar. It's an essential aspect of a visitor's experience. Nowadays, they have an intuitive search algorithm that's helped their company dominate the vacation booking market. But they didn't start out with this.

Back when they first launched their website, around 2008,

Airbnb had no idea what kind of data they should provide their customers with, so they settled on a basic search algorithm that collected the highest quality listings within a given radius of where the user searched.

As Airbnb acquired more and more customer data, their search algorithm gradually improved—serving more relevant results to customers based on their past booking history and search behavior.

Then in 2014, Airbnb leveraged their consumer testing data to uncover a usability problem that was occurring in certain Asian countries.[21] They noticed bookings were considerably lower in certain demographic regions, and a data scientist on their team discovered that a navigation menu tab titled "Neighborhood" was distracting users from engaging with the home page search bar (the primary route to booking). Users would visit the Neighborhood page, get lost in a sea of photos, and eventually leave—never returning to the site to complete a booking.

To solve this problem, Airbnb ran a simple test (remember, bigger tests don't equal bigger results). They removed the Neighborhood link from their navigation menu and highlighted the top travel destinations in China, Korea, Japan,

---

21   Max Song and Carl Shan, "How Airbnb Used Data to Propel Its Growth to a $10B Valuation," VentureBeat, May 18, 2014, https://venturebeat.com/2014/05/18/how-airbnb-used-data-to-propel-its-growth-to-a-10b-valuation/.

and Singapore instead—encouraging users to search for listings located near these destinations.

This simple adjustment to their home page resulted in a 10 percent lift in conversions from their Asian site visitors.

Nowadays, Airbnb continues to perfect their user experience through careful, iterative testing. Rather than undergoing a complete redesign every several years, they rely on incremental adjustments to optimize the usability and efficiency of their website.

Every website has the potential to be further optimized, and at no point should you see your site as "complete" or "good enough." If Airbnb had that mentality, it probably wouldn't have become the household name it is today.

THE 1 PERCENT RULE: HOW TO GET BETTER AND STAY BETTER

Instead of thinking of your conversion rate as a thirty-day get-rich-quick scheme, think of it like a 401(k) plan. The goal of a 401(k) is to encourage you to allocate a small percentage of each paycheck toward your retirement. Over time, those small payments compound, and you're left with a sizable nest egg to retire on. The earlier you start, the larger your compounded savings will be. The same principle applies to optimizing your website's conversion rate:

the sooner you can start making marginal improvements, the greater the benefits you'll see over time.

the PoweR of TiNy GAiNS

1% BetteR EveRy DAY $\quad 1.01^{365} = 37.78$

1% WoRse EveRy DAY $\quad 0.99^{365} = 0.03$

1 year

In the book *Atomic Habits*,[22] author James Clear makes a strong case for why these marginal gains tend to provide for better results in the long term. Let's say you maintain a daily improvement of 1 percent to any specific aspect of

---

22   James Clear, *Atomic Habits: An Easy & Proven Way to Build Good Habits & Break Bad Ones* (New York: Avery, 2018).

your website. If you get 1 percent each day, for an entire year, you'll be thirty-seven times better by the time you're done. Thirty-seven! You may not notice the ripples the first few improvements generate, but compounded over time, those small wins and ripples will build into a tidal wave of conversions for your business.

For an e-commerce site, this can look like collecting qualitative user data and combing through it for simple improvement ideas. You predict what improvements will help, then test those predictions through experiments. You learn from the experiment, make a winning improvement, and move on to the next most crucial area. It's an iterative process like this that compounds to produce big results.

Keep in mind, how quickly you optimize is dependent on how fast you can learn and implement. The quicker you create an iterative testing procedure, the faster you'll be able to make improvements to your website. So ditch the silver bullet mindset and the notion that one big win (like one flashy player) will instantly recoup your investment. Big one-time wins rarely happen, and businesses that shoot for the moon often end up wasting their time and money without achieving measurable success (they miss the moon and burn fuel floating around in space). Don't make that mistake. Take the *Moneyball* and Amazon approach instead. Conversion rate optimization is a process based on iteration, and scientific experimentation is how you make it work.

CHAPTER 3

LAW: NEW VISITORS ARE AT YOUR SITE FOR TWO REASONS

Big idea: Visitors are only at your site for one of two reasons. Your job is to help them get what they came for.

Once net new visitors reach your e-commerce site, your marketing's already won. Marketing got the visitor there by building awareness, driving traffic, and crafting a compelling value proposition. Now your website's job is to sell—to help potential customers get what they came for, which is one of two things:

1. **To research your products** and understand if these can solve their pain or need

2. **To purchase** as quickly and effortlessly as possible

That's it. Those are the two reasons new visitors are at your site.

And although there are hundreds of ways a visitor's journey to each goal can play out, the destinations are the same: research or buy. This means every website optimization you make should focus on removing friction to these two paths:

1. **Research a product or product type**
    A. Make it clear how your product will make the consumer's life better (clear value proposition)
    B. Support effortless research (clear pathways)
    C. Support visitors who have specific product questions
    D. Support multiple devices (mobile, tablet, desktop)
    E. Compare products/prices/features
    F. Dealer or store lookup
    G. Fit or size chart
2. **Purchase a product** and feel good about the decision
    A. Reduce in-cart objections and confusion (price, shipping, security)
    B. Support effortless purchase (in checkout)
    C. Have a helpful post-purchase flow (confirmation emails, easy support)
    D. Support effortless returns (boost confidence)

At its core, conversion rate optimization is about removing as much friction from a website experience as possible so nothing inhibits a consumer from researching and purchasing a product. This benefits the customer AND you—at the end of the day, you both want a conversion.

CHAPTER 4

LAW: ONCE VISITORS ARRIVE, STOP MARKETING TO THEM

Big idea: If you want more conversions, start treating your website like a sales channel, not a marketing channel.

Back in 2013, Forrester published two studies announcing we've entered the "age of the customer."[23] Power, they argued, has tipped away from businesses and suppliers and toward product purchasers. Here's a quick recap of the preceding ages and how the power shift has happened:

---

23   George Colony, Peter Burris, Kyle McNabb, and Andrew Smith, "Technology Management in the Age of the Customer," Forrester, October 10, 2013, https://www.forrester.com/report/Tec hnology+Management+In+The+Age+Of+The+Customer/-/E-RES103702; David Cooperstein, Alexandra Hayes, Elizabeth Ryckewaert, and Josh Bernoff, "Competitive Strategy in the Age of the Customer," Forrester, October 10, 2013, https://www.forrester.com/report/Competitive+Strategy +In+The+Age+Of+The+Customer/-/E-RES59159?objectid=RES59159.

- **Age of Manufacturing (1900–1960):** Shopping was concentrated in local stores or mail catalogs. Businesses controlled what information customers saw and how they purchased.
- **Age of Distribution (1960–1990):** We got better at moving things around the country and world, and this meant goods began traveling widely. In this age, the scales of power tipped even heavier to businesses. They still controlled information flow and the purchasing process, and they now had more margin for error—a larger consumer base meant businesses could afford more mistakes. Customer satisfaction frequently took a back seat.
- **Age of Information (1990–2010):** As the internet became more accessible (via browsers and affordable home computers), consumers started tipping the scales in the other direction—toward them. They were no longer at the sole mercy of what businesses told them; they could research plentiful reviews and compare a wide variety of products more freely. Businesses still held a lot of power but less than they had in the prior two ages.

Since then, the power shift toward consumers has only accelerated. In fact, it's been a bit of a landslide. These days, we don't just have five or ten places to purchase clothes online; we have five thousand. And thanks to social media, we can immediately tell five hundred or (for the more popular among us) five thousand of our friends whether we loved or hated the place we shopped that day. Businesses aren't completely stripped of their power, of course, but they're no longer the star of the commerce show. The problem is, many e-commerce sites operate like they're still the ringleader and still have the margin for error businesses enjoyed in the age of distribution. To put it plainly, they're stuck in the past.

One aspect of this "old age" thinking is particularly troublesome to me. It's this: Many brands I meet treat their e-commerce site as a marketing channel and put it under a marketer's jurisdiction. You may wonder, "What's so problematic about this?" And the answer is, it's problematic because marketers tend to approach a website from a brand perspective. They have objectives, priorities, and key performance indicators (KPIs) that are brand-centric. Big-picture, this means when a marketer is in charge of an e-commerce site, brand goals are prioritized over customer goals.

Here's what this looks like when you zoom in close. When marketers write product descriptions, they often sell the lifestyle or overall brand vision of the company but not how the particular product meets the visitor's individual needs. Think "our iconic logo hat in blue" (self-serving) versus "our closer-fitting trucker hat has an organic cotton front, a polyester mesh back, and an adjustable snap closure" (targets an eco-conscious, sporty customer with a few compelling reasons to buy). When you extrapolate this brand-centric approach to every other part of an e-commerce site, the result is an underperforming channel that values style over substance.

So what's a better option? Consider what would happen if e-commerce sites fell under the sales department instead. The user experience would be completely different (and, I'd argue, for the better!). Whereas marketing focuses on generating awareness, interest, and desire, sales focuses on conversions—getting out of the way once the visitor is ready to buy. This aligns much more closely with what your website should be doing.

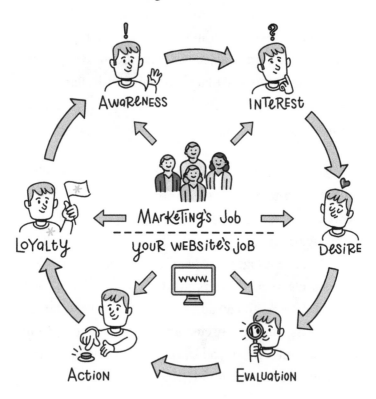

From many years of working with e-commerce brands both large and small, I've noticed the most successful brands acknowledge this split and actually do put their e-commerce site under a more sales-focused role. In many cases, this means a brand has at least the following roles:

- **A marketing manager** responsible for generating interest and awareness and driving good-fit visitors to the website.
- **An e-commerce manager** who oversees what happens when the visitor arrives. This role operates more like sales than marketing.

These separate but collaborative roles work together (like in the circular image above) to effectively get a visitor to the site and then get out of their way once they're there.

MARKETING MANAGERS VERSUS E-COMMERCE MANAGERS

At first glance, these roles sound pretty similar. But done well, they have a different set of responsibilities and KPIs:

ROLE	MARKETING MANAGER	E-COMMERCE MANAGER
RESPONSIBILITIES	• Traffic acquisition and ad management • Branding guidelines and voice • Content production • Search engine optimization • Social media accounts • Internal communications • Sales campaigns	• Information architecture and website navigation • Collecting user reviews • Website copy • Visual design and imagery (following branding guidelines) • Tech stack management • Site functionality
KPIS	• Return on ad spending (ROAS) • Media spend over net revenue	• Conversion rates • Site speed and uptime • Average order value • Product mix

Although brands differ on some role specifics, such as who creates the copy for each page on the website, the consensus is that the website is the e-commerce manager's domain.

Jeremy Horowitz, previously e-commerce manager at LuMee (a Case-Mate brand and distributor of phone cases) and now partner at Messenger Mastermind, says, "As the e-com manager, I was much more focused on the sales side of things...CRO, promotional calendar, website/tech stack management." He notes the website was the e-commerce manager's jurisdiction, though marketing played a heavy role in copy.

At Kuru Footwear, a growing brand with thirty-five employees, the website is also under an e-commerce manager. They have various channel managers on the marketing side, but CMO Sean McGinnis says when it comes to the website, "every design choice and every optimization is his [the e-commerce manager's] call." As a result, site uptime, speed, and site conversion rate are the e-commerce manager's responsibility as well.

Both of these brands—as well as some of the most successful brands The Good works with—recognize that yes, a marketing manager plays a critical role in driving the target audience to the site and amping up their interest before they get there. But once the visitor arrives, a handoff occurs. The visitor has crossed a boundary line, so to speak, and entered into the e-commerce manager's realm.

YOUR IT TEAM IS CRITICAL, BUT THEY SHOULDN'T BE IN CHARGE OF YOUR SITE EITHER

IT or web dev roles should also *not* be in charge of your e-commerce website. These technical roles are critical for making sure your store gets up, stays running, and remains secure (please don't neglect your hosting, code quality, security certifications, and other technical details!). But the responsibilities of your IT team should not extend to dictating how a customer moves through the site.

When a customer's path is dictated by an IT team, it often has the following friction points: too many available paths with little direction, abundant obstacles in the form of web trends or best practices (see rotating carousels), or a navel-gazing structure dictated by stakeholders.

Paul Irvine, an interim CIO/CTO consultant and self-proclaimed IT person, agrees. He recalls one instance where he was building an events startup and created a website for it. He said, "I had asked some early alpha testers to check my site out...and the first response was, 'I don't see how I add a new event?'" Paul was so focused on making the site flexible that he'd "buried the #1 basic reason someone would go there...to add an event!"

User experience (UX) and IT are often hard to reconcile under one role. The developer knows how the site functions (they coded the functionality, after all), but that makes it nearly impossible to know what the experience of the new-to-file user will be. It takes a special person, dedicated to user-centered practices, to create a website that isn't adversarial—that person isn't on your IT team.

OTHER REASONS AN E-COMMERCE SITE SHOULD BE THE E-COMMERCE MANAGER'S DOMAIN

Even for small, emerging brands with limited resources, hiring a dedicated e-commerce role whose job is to connect marketing needs with user needs, user research, and website optimization will result in a more focused website experience.

Expecting a marketing manager to pull off a successful marketing strategy *and* a successful conversion rate strategy is an enormous, unrealistic ask. You wouldn't expect an e-commerce expert to know the ins and outs of executing a successful marketing strategy, so why assume a marketer could do the same in an e-commerce role? Marketers who are expected to do both will either pick one out of necessity or stretch themselves too thin across both domains (i.e., do both poorly).

At The Good, we see this conflict in action in reporting metrics, where marketing managers turn canaries into KPIs. Starting in the early 1900s, miners took caged canaries down into the shafts. Canaries are more sensitive to gases like carbon monoxide (deadly in high doses) than humans. If a canary suddenly seemed ill (or worse, died), miners knew it was high time to hightail it back to open air.

In reporting, modern-day canaries are metrics that indicate some larger, dangerous issue is at work. Take "time on page" or "time on-site." If you're testing different landing pages and visitors are bouncing after nine seconds, you may have a terrible top-of-page experience. Alternatively, this metric can be a clue to a larger mystery.

In one instance, the team at The Good noticed visitors were somehow arriving on the cart page from every kind of channel. But this was theoretically impossible; you can't get to the cart through paid search. What the team found was visitors spent a lot of time on-site doing research and then moved off-site to find missing information or a coupon code. By the time the visitor returned, their session had timed out,[24] and it appeared as if they just arrived on the cart page.

Time on page is useful as a canary. But marketing often treats this and similar metrics, such as pageviews, as KPIs. This isn't throwaway data, but it doesn't reveal nearly as much as return on ad spend (ROAS), average order value (AOV), conversion rate (CR), and other essential e-commerce metrics that reveal a good deal more about how the customer is experiencing the site.

THINK OF YOUR SITE LIKE A BRICK-AND-MORTAR STORE

Many brands have online experiences they wouldn't dare put customers through if they were looking them eye to eye in a retail store. Yet, just because you can't see the customer across the screen, it doesn't mean you should treat them worse. To curb these "out of sight, out of mind" experiences,

---

24 Google Analytics will time out a visitor's session after thirty minutes of inactivity.

think of your e-commerce store as a brick-and-mortar store. Any website that sells products or services is a store, and you can apply the same principles behind creating a successful brick-and-mortar retail space to designing your website.

Imagine you're traveling to a new city. You have an hour to spare, so you pop into a local boutique. Two steps past the door, just as soon as your eyes have adjusted to the bright store lighting, an employee interrupts your stride with a "great deal," a 10 percent discount toward your first purchase in exchange for your email address. After you get over your initial surprise, you'd probably feel a bit accosted (you don't even know if you want anything in the store yet!), and this experience would negatively impact your overall impression of the store. Best case, you keep shopping at a safe distance with one eye out for the overly eager employee. Worst case, you leave on the spot. Neither is an ideal outcome for the store. But for some reason, e-commerce businesses use this exact tactic to capture email addresses and entice visitors to complete a purchase right when a consumer hits their site ("Sign up for our email list and receive 10 percent off your first order!"). Worse, many e-commerce stores go so far as to position "guards" at the door—exit pop-ups—that prevent customers from leaving easily. Imagine leaving a retail store and having an associate bar your exit!

Although brands justify this behavior online, it's even more detrimental there than it'd be in person. For one, what consumers perceive as irritating in a retail store is amplified when shopping online. The average amount of time a visitor spends on the *top* US e-commerce sites is around four minutes,[25] and their patience during that time is at an absolute minimum. (Keep in mind, this average is for sites customers recognize and, to a certain extent, already trust.) For another, these tactics are so prevalent that most visitors have been subconsciously trained to blow past them. So the tactic is not only annoying; it's also largely ineffective.

KEEP IN MIND: DEFECTION LATENCY

"Hey, those kinds of pop-ups work for us," some brands argue, "and they collect a LOT of email addresses!" This may be true in the immediate term—as in, yes, you add a pop-up and collect more emails. But keep in mind, this "gain" doesn't happen in a vacuum; it's like a drop of dye in a glass of water. It ripples out and colors the visitor's entire perception of the brand.

For this reason, many changes may look like a success in a spreadsheet but have serious effects on the visitor's overall journey. Rishi Rawat, CEO at Frictionless Commerce, calls

---

25   Stephanie Chevalier, "Leading U.S. Online Retail Properties by Average Session Duration 2018," Statista, July 7, 2021, https://www.statista.com/statistics/790897/unique-visitors-average-session-durations-retail-properties-us/.

this *defection latency*[26]—the gap between when you make a change and when you see downstream effects.

You can see a classic example of defection latency when brands ramp up their email frequency.[27] Oftentimes, brands note a correlation between more emails and more purchases. Managers lean into this correlation and steadily ramp up email sends (it puts them closer to their KPI, after all), even when customers begin saying, "Whoa, hey, too many promos!" Yet, managers press through this feedback because even though the customer is saying one thing, the data still indicates more emails = more purchases.

That is, until the day the brand accrues an enormous unsubscribe rate. (To say nothing of all the emails landing in promotions or spam and lowering the credibility of the sender's address.) At this point, a large percentage of customers have defected, and the brand has seriously damaged a critical channel (email returns an average of thirty-five dollars for every one dollar spent[28]). This is defection latency, and it's important to keep in mind when you're considering how a singular change impacts the overall customer experience.

---

26 Rishi Rawat, "Be Aware of Adoption/Defection Latency," *Frictionless Commerce* (blog), November 21, 2020, https://www.frictionless-commerce.com/blog/be-aware-of-adoption-defection-latency/.

27 Rawat provides an example here: https://www.youtube.com/watch?v=L-HHx_KUcHg.

28 From a survey of 236 respondents who work in marketing in the United Kingdom. https://dma.org.uk/uploads/ckeditor/marketer_email_tracker/Marketer_email_tracker_2020.pdf.

Back to our hour-to-kill-in-a-new-city trip. Let's say you wound up leaving that odd boutique and decided you could use a pick-me-up before your next meeting. Google Maps says there's a coffee shop right around the corner, so you beeline toward some caffeine. The café has a welcoming exterior, and the first thing that hits your nose when you walk in is the smell of fresh-roasted coffee beans—a good sign. But as you walk toward the counter, you notice something about the layout feels, well, off.

For one, the menu board isn't above the counter; it's above the door you walked in. The barista can see it much better than you can. Weird. Also, it's infuriating to read. You want to find the price of a black cup of coffee, but the board starts with three paragraphs about the café's history, followed by a list of the employees' favorite drinks that month, next to an elaborate version of their logo, which a local artist has added a seasonal flair to. After sixty seconds of skimming, you give up and figure you'll just ask the barista. It can't be *that* expensive, right? The barista smiles and waves you over. But before you can even ask, he launches into a rehearsed pitch. "Hi! Did you know our coffee shop only works with direct fair trade relationships and..." Geez, you think, what is *with* this city?

It's a painful example, but it's painfully close to what many brands do online.

When visitors land in many digital stores, they see a navigation structure centered on the brand: it has tabs such as "About Us," "Our Story," "Press," and "Testimonials." This is much like the self-serving and poorly organized coffee menu that made you work to find the very thing you came for (which, 99.99 percent of the time, is not the brand story). Compare that structure to an effective café menu, organized with sections such as *Classics*, *Specialty Drinks*, and *Tea*. Or compare it to an effective e-commerce menu, such as the one vitamin supplement company Bare Performance Nutrition has. In their main navigation, they organize their vitamins around *Weight Loss*, *Performance*, *Build Muscle*, and *Overall Health*, aka what goals their customers are looking to achieve by using their supplements!

Just like the best retail experiences are arranged to help customers quickly find what they need, the best e-commerce stores are organized to help customers research and purchase ASAP. Care about your customers' goals online instead of trying to convince them to care about your brand story.

BRAND GOALS VERSUS CUSTOMER GOALS

You may be picking up on the theme here. The poorest in-person and online experiences put the brand front and center; the best in-person and online experiences put the customer front and center. The best experiences make the customer feel seen, heard, and helped. This is intentional.

Successful brick-and-mortar stores know that serving the customer is how you serve the brand. (Case and point: 82 percent of buyers make a repeat purchase after brands make them feel known.[29]) This is a massive overarching parallel to online experiences, but it's one of the biggest similarities e-commerce stores miss.

The heart of this misunderstanding often boils down to one thing: believing brand goals (e.g., increase sales and customer touchpoints) are at odds with customer goals (research and purchase). Managers feel they must choose one or the other. So they choose brand goals, partly because stakeholders often have a louder microphone than customers and partly because managers are *incentivized* to put the brand above the customer.

However, customer goals aren't so different from brand goals as stakeholders or managers initially think. Take a look at how two common brand goals look when you put them in a customer context:

Brand Goal: Increase site revenue.

Customer Solution: Make it easier for customers to research and purchase products.

---

29   "45 Ecommerce Stats for Accelerated Digital Transformation," Gladly (2021), https://f.hubspotusercontent10.net/hubfs/2771217/Gladly-45-Stats-2021%20(1).pdf.

Brand Goal: Increase returning customer conversion.

Customer Solution: Personalize site for returning visitors and make it simple for returning customers to find and purchase products they are interested in quickly.

The brand still wins, right? What's more, focusing on the customer in these scenarios actually makes it *more* likely the brand will reach its goals. That's why the objective of your e-commerce strategy should be to create a website that prioritizes customer goals over brand goals.

The menu/navigation example I used earlier is a good illustration of this, but the customer-first mindset doesn't stop at the high-level organization. Here's a more granular example. Many clients come to The Good because they're running Google shopping ads. These ads often drive visitors to a product page. Sometimes, that specific product isn't what the visitor is looking for. On a brand-focused website, the visitor's journey ends there; they don't see what they need, and they leave, even though the brand very likely has a make, model, size, or style that would suit the visitor. Customer-focused websites, on the other hand, provide what we call directional guidance. They say something along the lines of, "Not what you're looking for? Right this way to other options." This guidance directs the customer to another part of the site and lowers the barrier to finding the right item. This helps the customer (they find an item) and the brand (they make a sale) alike.

So helping customers helps you—and not just when it comes to reaching big metrics either. Internally, putting the customer first can help teams, too. For example, shifting the focus to your customers' goals will help your team to engage in fewer debates of opinion (he wants it this way vs. she wants it that way). In a brand-focused environment, the ideas that get tested come from the person with the highest title or most influence. In a customer-focused environment, the ideas that get tested are ones that help the customer the most. The customer's well-being becomes the North Star, not the ego of the highest-paid team member. This benefits everyone.

UNCOVERING CUSTOMER GOALS: FINDING CLUES ONLINE

The Good's Director of CRO and UX Strategy, Natalie Thomas, once worked in retail sales for Stumptown Coffee Roasters. Reading people was an essential part of that job. She recalls, "I would know the relationship between two people who walked into my café before they said a word." From the customer's body language, to who paid and ordered, to the type of words they said, these indicators all told Natalie who was in the store. "There're so many clues," she says, "about who's the boss and who's the employee or dynamics like that, before they even get to the counter and speak a word to me." Natalie would read these clues to figure out what customers were looking for, how she could help, and how to speak their language.

Online, you don't have these body language clues. Visitors can't flag down an associate like they would in Restoration Hardware and say, "Hey, are these candles soy or petroleum?" And as the store owner or associate, you don't know whether the visitor is in a business suit or a sweatsuit, carrying a tourist map or car keys. But that doesn't mean you have nothing to go on. Natalie says there are plenty of clues online, too. You just have to know where to look. "Online, we have to look at the actions that they're actually taking, the places that they're falling off, the rage clicks, the search terms," she says, and use those to figure out what the customer's goals are.

Most of this comes down to paying attention and listening. Listening to search queries that pour in through the search bar (or your chatbot). Listening to the emails your customer support team gets. Paying attention to the first three pages they visit and what browser, device, and channel they come from. Looking at heatmaps of what they do on each page. All of these are clues telling you what visitors want. In a sense, visitors leave a scent trail that you should be able to pick up and react to if you're paying attention.

Does this look exactly the same as brick and mortar? No,

of course not. But it's more similar than brands think. In both a retail store and an online store, the customers give abundant clues as to why they're there and what they want.

REMINDER: ONLINE HAS PLENTY OF UNIQUE ADVANTAGES

Not seeing customers can feel like operating with one arm tied behind your back. But online provides plenty of other opportunities and advantages.

Consider the beauty industry. If a visitor were looking for blush in a retail beauty store—say, Ulta—the main ways to try those blushes is to either (A) pick some and take them home or (B) walk around the store for an hour and swatch various shades on their hand to assess sheen, consistency, and pigmentation. And really, neither option is ideal. Option A is a shot in the dark, and option B takes a considerable amount of time, plus your hand isn't quite the same as your cheek.

Online provides a better alternative. In their app, Ulta lets visitors virtually try on makeup via AR technology called GLAMlab. Using access to the shopper's camera, the app shows the shopper what each shade of blush looks like on their face. It's fast, effective, and a great example of where online can surpass in-person experiences.

And again, helping the customer helps the brand here. According to Kelly Mahoney, Ulta's Vice President of Customer Marketing, the live try-on feature called GLAMlab had nine times more engagement in 2020 than its previous most-engaged metric.[30] And although other factors were certainly at play, e-commerce sales grew 90 percent year-over-year from 2019 to 2020.

DON'T MAKE YOUR VISITORS THINK

Your website isn't simply a marketing platform for your brand. It's a virtual store for your audience to buy directly from you. Once your customers are on-site (in your store), your marketing has won. Beyond that point, your main focus is serving their needs—making your store as usable and pleasant as possible for your specific visitors trying to reach specific goals. To do this well, you'll need to shift your thinking about your store and start looking at that e-commerce manager role.

You'll also need to close the gap between how you *think* folks use their website and how they actually do. Steve Krug, author of *Don't Make Me Think*,[31] points out, "When we're creating sites, we act as though people are going to

---

30   Stephanie Crets, "Ulta Loyalty Members Drive 95% of Sales," Digital Commerce 360, January 18, 2021, https://www.digitalcommerce360.com/2021/01/18/ulta-loyalty-members-drive-95-of-sales/.

31   Steve Krug, *Don't Make Me Think* (Berkeley, CA: New Riders Press, 2000).

pore over each page, reading our finely crafted text, figuring out how we've organized things, and weighing their options before deciding which link to click." But that's not at all what happens. (Remember, the average time a visitor spends on an e-commerce site is four minutes—at best.) Krug goes on to say, "What they actually do most of the time (if we're lucky) is *glance* at each new page, scan *some* of the text, and click on the first link that catches their interest or vaguely resembles the thing they're looking for." Put another way, we treat a website like a monumental thesis or some great work of brand literature, whereas a visitor's interaction with it is more like driving past a billboard on the highway. Or popping into a local coffee shop for a black cup of coffee.

Remember, your customers are visiting for one of two reasons: to research or purchase. An effective conversion rate optimization plan is about removing barriers to those goals and getting them to where they want to go. And so, much like in brick-and-mortar stores, aligning your e-commerce site with your visitors' needs is the single best way to drive more conversions, revenue, and other key metrics.

CHAPTER 5

LAW: YOU CAN'T READ THE LABEL FROM INSIDE THE JAR

Big idea: You can't understand the new-to-file experience—you're too close to your brand. Luckily, there are a few ways to fix that.

In 2020, ESPN released a documentary on Michael Jordan called *The Last Dance*. It's a fascinating study on excellence. One theme that runs through all ten episodes of the documentary is this: greatness casts a long, dark shadow.

Michael Jordan's relentless drive to be the best, to create and defy all rivalries, played a key role in his rise to the greatest basketball player of all time. He refused failure. He put in extra training hours. He invented competitions and rivalries (where none existed!) to raise the bar higher and higher. It worked. Jordan rode his ambition to astonishing heights and global fame.

But this immense strength had a flip side, and it's one the documentary doesn't ignore. Jordan's relentless drive and extreme competitiveness didn't just factor into his success; it also contributed to fractured relationships with his teammates, family, and himself. The last scene of *The Last Dance* (warning: spoiler ahead) is a red-eyed Jordan sitting alone in his 56,000-square-foot mansion with stiff knees, a smoldering cigar, and memories of all that he's won—and traded. It's haunting.

This "great strengths cast great shadows" idea isn't a new concept or one that's unique to MJ. In most (perhaps every) towering leader—whether it's on a basketball court, in an art studio, or in a boardroom—you see this conflict. Michael Jordan, Floyd Mayweather Jr., Pablo Picasso, Steve Jobs... their great strengths had equally great weaknesses.

And even though you and I may not stand on the same heights as those folks, the same is true of us. Our greatest strengths are often our biggest weaknesses. Where there's an Achilles, there's an Achilles' heel as well.

What does this have to do with e-commerce retailers?

When it comes to your e-commerce store, one of your biggest strengths is your perspective—how well you know your store, products, and competitors. You're an expert on those things. But this strength casts a shadow, and the shadow is this: you no longer know what it's like to see your store and products for the first time. Your perspective into the store also serves as your blinders; you can't see what a new-to-file experience is like for someone outside the store.

You're stuck inside the jar, so to speak, and there's no way to read the label from in there.

WHAT STUCK INSIDE THE JAR LOOKS LIKE FOR E-COMMERCE RETAILERS

Think about that image for a minute. You're sitting inside a drained jar of pickles (or jam, or whatever jarred item you prefer). Smooth, glass walls tower around you, and the backside of the label is blocking out some light. You've shrunk, of course, and you can see the label has letters—perhaps you can string a few of them together or guess what a word or two is from the lingering smell inside the jar—but no matter where you stand, you can't get a clear picture of that label.

Is it the kind of label that catches your eye on a stocked store shelf? Does it evoke a homey sense, like something your grandma would have in her pantry? Is it a confusing mishmash of jargon ("a proprietary blend of non-GMO and

cruelty-free ingredients, from our earth to your shelves")
that leaves consumers scratching their heads as to what,
exactly, is in the jar anyhow?

You don't know, and you can't tell from where you sit. Stuck
inside the jar means you're inside the brand, and it's impossible to have an unbiased perspective of how an "I've never
seen this before" visitor perceives it.

This is important because where we sit not only shapes
what we see, but it also shapes what we think, what we
say, and what we do ("your thoughts become your words,
your words become your actions, your actions become your
habits" and all that jazz). Meaning, a retailer that sits inside
the jar builds from inside the jar, too. And this makes for
some very confusing e-commerce websites:

- **Category dropdowns** that organize product the way
  retailers would in a warehouse
- **Filters** that use jargon like "classic performance tech"
  instead of visitor-friendly words such as "running shirts"
- **Navigations** that revolve around the brand and its awe-
  someness
- **Product descriptions** that focus on manufacturing
  details instead of customer benefits
- **Site paths** built around the retailer's understanding of
  the products and competitors, not around visitors who
  are unfamiliar with both

- **Websites** that serve brand goals first and help consumers second

And many other related missteps that make a lot of sense to retailers but no sense to the visitor.

HOW CONFIRMATION BIAS MAKES YOU EVEN MORE STUCK

This would be less of an issue if retailers realized that they are, in fact, stuck. But many don't.

Part of the reason for this is confirmation bias (you've probably heard of it). Confirmation bias is the human tendency to seek out and grab on to information that confirms one's own beliefs and values. Like a child who insists all autumn leaves are yellow and picks up only the yellow leaves in the backyard to prove it.

When we act on confirmation bias, we behave like the insistent child. We leave all the red, brown, green, and orange leaves lying where they fell and only pick up leaves that fit our perspective. We cherry-pick evidence that proves our beliefs and, by necessity, reject information that conflicts or challenges our point of view. (I use "we" and "our" here because I'm as prone to this bias as you are!)

One reason we do this is that we take in an enormous

amount of information each day. We also face a flood of seemingly endless and small decisions. How much coffee to pour? Cream and sugar? Check Twitter or no? Like the tweet or not? What to say to that text? Bathroom break now or later? To navigate this immense cognitive load, our brains have biases, or small glitches, in our thinking. In many ways, those glitches are helpful—they create short-cuts and prevent total brain overload. But in other ways, those glitches are harmful—they drive us to inaccurate and damaging conclusions.

Here's how this looks for some retailers. I often talk with managers who run surveys. This is, in theory, a great prac-tice and one I encourage. But they taint how effective surveying is by asking leading questions. For example, "How much do you love our product?" or "How much do you love this feature on a scale from one to ten?" These brands *think* they're doing customer research, and they *think* they're getting a better picture of their visitors. In reality, they're using surveys and research to gather evi-dence for a belief the brand already holds. They're asking, "How many yellow leaves do you see?" The question is engi-neered to confirm the bias the asker holds—for example, to confirm all autumn leaves are yellow or all customers do, in fact, love the product.

The better approach is one that keeps confirmation bias at a distance. This primarily involves asking less biased questions, such as "What color leaves do you see?" Or, in the context of our retail example, "Tell me how you use this product." When The Good researches how visitors experience an e-commerce site, we ask questions such as "What would you come here for?" or "What do you think you can do on this website?"

Note that we don't start with "What can you buy here?" There's a reason for that. Although it seems like a harmless question, it's a leading one because not every site makes it clear you can shop there. Let that soak in a minute. It may be clear to you your site is an e-commerce store, but it's entirely possible visitors don't know you're selling products at all.

WHAT THIS PAINT BRAND DIDN'T KNOW

We once worked with a brand that sold environmentally conscious paint products through wholesale partners (e.g., Home Depot). They also offered direct-to-consumer sales through their e-commerce website. However, their e-commerce team was seeing a high bounce rate and conversions they weren't happy with. So they approached The Good.

To start, we conducted user testing and observed how real customers navigated the site. What we found surprised us.

The website's home page prominently displayed logos of retail partners that stocked the brand's paint, as well as logos of reputable media sources that praised their products. The brand's thought process was this: if consumers knew a reputable retailer carried the paint products, consumers would think, "This brand is legit; I'll buy from them!"

The logos were also supposed to work in combination with the site-wide navigation menu, which focused less on products and more on educating visitors about the paint brand. The items in the brand's original navigation menu included:

- Shop
- Learn
- Blog
- Projects
- Certifications
- FAQ

The problem was, visitors didn't arrive and think, "Wow! They're credible. Let me snag some paint while I'm here." Nope. Website visitors saw the big-box logos and immediately assumed the website provided manufacturer information—*not* products through an e-commerce store. Visitors didn't even realize they could buy something! They thought they needed to go to a physical retail store to do that. And so, the company was missing out on loads of online sales.

Once we gathered this out-of-the-jar perspective, we knew how to help. Our team's highest priority became testing the menu and creating a more shopping-focused version.

Along with removing the wholesale partner logos, we ultimately redesigned their site-wide menu to focus on products rather than the brand. The items in the brand's revised navigation menu included:

- Paints
- Primers
- Stain & Varnish
- Concrete Products
- Samples

After implementing this variation on the brand's website, we saw an immediate improvement in on-site engagement and conversions. By shifting focus away from the brand, we provided a way for visitors to discover more about the products and move through the sales funnel more efficiently.

This is a prime example of why fresh perspective matters. From the brand's perspective, there weren't any glaring problems with their store. It wasn't until *after* we performed user testing and identified what customers were saying that they could see the underlying issues hindering sales.

This paint brand thought they were selling paint through their online store. But when we asked visitors what they'd do with the site, they said, "Use it to find fact sheets." If we had started with the question, "What would you buy on this site?" our conversations with site visitors may have been very different and far less helpful.

SO WHAT? WHY GETTING OUTSIDE THE JAR IS WELL WORTH THE EFFORT

IF YOU'RE NOT HELPING CUSTOMERS REACH THEIR GOALS, YOU'RE NOT REACHING YOURS EITHER

Remember, visitors come to your site for one of two reasons. The first is to **research** your brand's products and understand if they solve their pain or need. The second is to **convert** and purchase your brand's products, once they're convinced you can solve their pain or need.

If a consumer doesn't understand your website, how to navigate it, what products you're selling, or even that you are selling products, they won't be able to accomplish either goal. The correlation? You won't accomplish your goals either—goals such as increasing revenue, average order value, return on ad spending, and many more. The only healthy, sustainable way to hit those goals is by helping visitors achieve their goals. It may sound cliché, but it's true: when they win, you do, too. Put another way, your goals and your visitor's goals are aligned: you both want a conversion.

Take American Express. They invested in understanding their customers and improving processes. As a result, they saw a 400 percent increase in customer retention.[32] What's more, as American Express put customer success as the core of their strategy, they were able to move into other aspects of the customer's life as well, such as travel and entertainment. When the customer wins, the brand does, too.

YOU HAVE TO STEP OUTSIDE THE JAR TO KNOW WHAT TO TEST

When you're suffering from stuck-inside-the-jar syndrome, you don't have the tools to fix the problem above; you're not equipped to help site visitors to win—even if you want. If you try and test improvements, you're going to test in one of two ways:

- **Option A:** You won't test at all because you believe your store is fine or good enough.
- **Option B:** You'll randomly test the improvements *you* think will help. You'll test around your gut interests, reactions, inspirations, or stakeholder suggestions.

Option B may deliver some minor improvements (you're

---

32 "Road to Excellence: How American Express Leads the Way for Customer Experience Transformation," Engage Customer, May 27, 2015, https://engagecustomer.com/road-to-excellence-how-american-express-leads-the-way-for-customer-experience-transformation/.

wearing blinders but aren't *totally* blind, after all) but not the compounding ones that generate significant revenue and returns. To do *that* kind of testing, you need (as we pointed out in Chapter 2, "The Scientific Method, Not Silver Bullets") better inputs than your gut, trends, or boardroom opinion. You need the customer's experience, which you only get from outside the jar.

So, where does all this leave brands? What's the point of knowing you're stuck and hurting conversions if you can't get unstuck?

It turns out, there are two ways to get outside the jar: hire someone to come and pull you out, or build a ladder yourself.

OPTION 1: HIRE SOMEONE TO PULL YOU OUT

Brands often come to The Good because we're a neutral third party. We offer the perspective of someone who's informed about conversion rate optimization but not biased.

This is particularly useful for teams who designed or approved the design for an e-commerce site. To be frank, those teams are the worst candidates for the job of conversion rate optimization, not because they're unintelligent, incompetent, or lazy (they're rarely any of those.) but because they bring a lot of unconscious or conscious biases to the work.

For example:

- **A CEO or owner may have a limiting presupposition of who their customers are and what visitors want from their website.** That mistake, no matter how passionately the owner believes it, will limit the company's sales and growth.
- **An e-commerce manager may have sunk dozens of hours into a feature that is tanking the conversion rate.** Seeing and admitting that mistake is the last thing that person wants to do. (This relates to the sunk cost fallacy, which is where we keep walking along a poor path simply because we've already invested time and resources in it.)
- **Someone who's looked at the same website every day for years may be missing obvious mistakes.** They may be incapable of perceiving any problems on their website because they've spent so much time with it. They are inside the jar.

Outsourcing optimization to a third-party expert is a fast and effective way to combat existing assumptions and unearth new opportunities your team may never have identified as a problem. It's like having someone reach down and pull you out of the jar.

The other option is to climb out yourself.

OPTION 2: BUILDING A LADDER TO CLIMB OUTSIDE THE JAR

If hiring someone to pull you out of the jar isn't an option (for financial or other reasons), your other choice is to build a ladder and climb out yourself. Of course, you need more than your bare hands and vertical prowess to do this. The walls are quite tall and slippery.

You need a ladder, and building one requires a few different steps.

1. ADMIT YOU DON'T KNOW WHAT YOU DON'T KNOW

The first step is acknowledging you don't understand your visitors' needs as well as you should. It's acknowledging that you are, indeed, stuck.

This is true *even if you've done extensive customer research.* I often meet brands that argue, "But we've already talked with our customers, and we know them pretty well. We don't need to do more research. We know what they need." These brands have taken an excellent first step that many other brands neglect, and I want to be careful to applaud their efforts. But their mistake is this: they believe customer and visitor research is a "one and done" thing.

Regardless of what industry you're in, market factors flux. The competitive landscape is constantly shifting. Tools and technology—and how both you and your customers use them—are always changing. Channel engagement rises and falls (Twitter today, TikTok tomorrow). National trends and opinions shift in a week or mere twenty-four hours. The world doesn't stand still, and it never has. Why would your consumers? They, too, are in a perpetual state of change.

Once you recognize this, you can start building your ladder.

2. FIND YOUR RAILS: PRIORITIZE THE CUSTOMER'S GOALS OVER YOURS

The first materials you want to gather are your rails. They're your visitors' goals, which are always to research and/or convert.

These goals are easy to find, but I didn't say they're easy to pick up. To be clear, I'm talking about a big priority shift here. Chances are, most of your KPIs are brand-centric, or franken-KPIs that attempt to serve the brand and customer equally well. Your new goal is to create a website that puts the needs of the website visitors first—exclusively.

Once again, this doesn't just benefit the customer. It benefits you, your teams, and your bottom line. Figuring out which ideas to test in your meetings probably looks a good bit like battle royale right now. There's no single source of truth (e.g., the customer's goals) in the decision room, so figuring out which ideas matter are often dictated by shifting and relative "truths" such as who's paid the most, has charisma, speaks the loudest, or brought doughnuts that day (hey, I've seen it all over a decade-plus of optimization). Orienting teams and organizations around the customer helps with this chaos. It gives teams a North Star and eliminates many of the conversations around whims, gut improvements, and ideas I had in the shower.

To do this kind of orienting, you'll need to consider:

1. **Top-level buy-in:** For individual teams to have the resources, tools, and processes they need to prioritize site visitor goals, the founder and senior leaders need to be on board with putting the customer first.

2. **Incentivizing customer-first actions:** From who you hire, to team KPIs, to bonus structures, individuals need to be incentivized to put the customer first. Actions follow incentives.

3. **Empowering customer-first experiences:** Incentives are a great start, but they only go so far if teams aren't equipped to meet those incentives. Point employees toward putting the customer first, then empower them to go and do it. Train them on what "customer first" looks like, give them authority to do "anything up to [x] to make visitors and customers succeed," and encourage them to share good experiences and lessons learned.

4. **Democratizing customer access:** This could look like Glossier's mandatory two-hour retail shifts for new hires[33] (literally putting employees in front of customers) or ensuring every employee does at least one day/hour at the support desk. It could also look like making sure all teams are equipped to do customer interviews or have access to customer data (appropriately anonymized).

3. GATHER YOUR RUNGS: PAY CLOSE ATTENTION TO WHAT YOUR VISITORS SAY AND DO

The next thing you need to do is gather some rungs to have on your rails. In principle, these are also easy to find: listen to your customers.

In practice, you'd be surprised how many online business owners and managers don't do this. When ProfitWell looked at over three thousand subscription companies, they found seven out of ten organizations are speaking to fewer than ten prospects per month in research conversations (i.e., ones that aren't sales).[34]

---

33 Glossier's SVP of Marketing, Ali Weiss, is credited with this idea. Kaleigh Moore, "How Glossier's New Employee Program Gathers Rich Customer Insight," *Forbes*, October 7, 2019, https://www.forbes.com/sites/kaleighmoore/2019/10/07/how-glossiers-new-employee-program-gathers-rich-customer-insight/?sh=52e8499e202d.

34 This was true for a wide range of subscription companies ranging from $0 to $50M+ in revenue. Patrick Campbell, "Customer Research: Benchmarks and Common Mistakes," ProfitWell, May 29, 2018, https://www.profitwell.com/recur/all/customer-research-benchmarks.

There are several reasons brands don't talk with customers as often as they should:

1. **They don't know they're stuck.** Brands don't acknowledge their perspective is problematic, and so they have little interest in a solution. As Amy Edmonson put it, "It's hard to learn if you already know."[35]
2. **They haven't prioritized the customer.** They may admit their perspective isn't perfect, but they haven't systemically fixed it.
3. **They don't know how.** They've heard they need an outside perspective and believe it. But they're stuck on any number of "how to do it" questions.

The first two points I addressed above. The third I can address here. Much like in real-life conversations, listening primarily means you do less talking and more noticing. Specifically, what the other person:

· Says and doesn't say
· Does and doesn't do

When it comes to your e-commerce store and the folks who visit it, there are two ways to listen for this information: quantitatively and qualitatively.

---

35 Via a popular Edmonson TED talk: https://www.ted.com/talks/
amy_edmondson_how_to_turn_a_group_of_strangers_into_a_team/transcript?language=en.

Quantitative listening largely involves observing visitor behavior for insights: analytics events, A/B testing, website chat logs, large-scale user surveys, heatmaps on FAQ pages (or all key pages, for that matter), and many more. The unifying goal of these activities is to understand what visitors are doing/not doing and saying/not saying. Think of this "active listening data" as your bottom rungs.

To add more rungs and climb further up the ladder and out of the jar, you'll want to dig into the why behind all of the what you uncovered in quantitative exploration. To dig into why, you want to do qualitative forms of listening. These include interviewing customers or potential visitors, as well as your team members who regularly interact with customers and visitors.

HOW LISTENING WELL HELPED EASTON SPORTS

Easton is the biggest manufacturer of baseball equipment in the world. Over 90 percent of college baseball swings rely on an Easton bat, and Easton is the official supplier for the Little League World Series.

But when Easton approached The Good, they were lagging in the direct-to-consumer sales market, specifically at the fifteen-year-old level. To find out why sales and conversions weren't better, The Good did some listening. We set up a simple

Google form, and we showed it to the customer service team. For two days, we asked them to fill out that form after every call with a potential customer. The form asked a few simple questions about the purpose of the call and how the service team member solved the complaint.

Listening to what the service team heard gave us a big clue. A lot of potential customers were calling in because they couldn't figure out the best bat for their child. When we looked at the product category page on Easton's site, this made sense. It was a wall of bats with little guidance on which one to choose. The product detail pages didn't help much either—they primarily listed technical details such as size, length, and how big around the bat was.

This may have made sense for visitors familiar with choosing a technical bat. Say, collegiate baseball players and college coaches. But it left most moms and dads of fifteen-year-olds scratching their heads. They had no idea which bats were approved for their child's league and what the differences were between technologies and price points.

Among other changes, we wound up designing a bat-finder questionnaire that helped visitors make a few easy selections to find the right bat for their kid. This quicker path to purchase (remember, visitors' two goals are to research and convert) resulted in a 240 percent increase in e-commerce revenue.

A FEW DIFFERENT WAYS TO LISTEN WELL

Listening and acting on visitor feedback is something any team can do. There is certainly no shortage of opportunities to listen in. Your customer service team, chatbot, email replies, social media tags, and more have all been aggregating plenty of qualitative data you can listen in on.

A good place to start is tapping into feedback that already exists—what your customer service team hears, for example—and opening up a feedback loop you can keep tapping into each month:

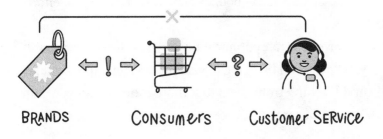

BRANDS   CONSUMers   Customer SERVICE

When you open up this loop (in addition to gaining clarity, testing confidence, and finding), you also add momentum to your conversion flywheel.

A flywheel is a good metaphor here because improving conversions won't happen in one push. It'll happen in many consecutive pushes. As Jim Collins explains in *Good to Great*, where he introduces the flywheel concept,[36] "Picture a

---

36   Jim Collins, *Good to Great* (New York: HarperCollins, 2001). Read a more detailed excerpt from Collin's book at https://www.jimcollins.com/concepts/the-flywheel.html.

huge, heavy flywheel—a massive metal disk mounted horizontally on an axle, about thirty feet in diameter, two feet thick, and weighing about 5,000 pounds. Now imagine that your task is to get the flywheel rotating on the axle as fast and long as possible." You give it a big push, and it moves a little. You keep pushing and it starts to move a little bit more. If you keep doing this in a consistent direction, "at some point—breakthrough! The momentum of the thing kicks in in your favor, hurling the flywheel forward, turn after turn... whoosh!...its own heavy weight working for you." Your pushing effort hasn't changed, but the wheel's speed has. And with each turn, it compounds both its speed and your efforts.

In conversion rate optimization turns, the more consistently you "push" on listening to visitors, testing improvements, and learning from them, the more momentum you gain, and the faster you accrue conversions.

So start by asking your customer service staff to describe a typical day for them, including the common issues and questions they resolve for customers. You'll be surprised by what you learn. (In almost every interview of a customer service team we've conducted, new and unexpected pain points have been exposed, and old issues that continue to plague customers have resurfaced.) Identify how you can address the issues you hear, test those issues, and learn from them. Lather, rinse, repeat, convert. Keep pushing on the flywheel.

THINK BIG, ACT SMALL

Imagine you're interviewing a site visitor (kudos for doing that) and they say something like, "You know what? I couldn't find boots in the navigation, so I just left." It's tempting to think "Aha! We need to add a boots category to the nav. Problem solved" and move on to the next conversation.

But this may or may not be the right solution. What your interviewee just voiced is a symptom. Your job is to treat that symptom as a clue that'll help you find the problem. If you have a headache, maybe you need blue light glasses because you're staring at screens for ten to twelve hours a day. Or a dental operation to deal with that aching tooth you've been trying to ignore. Or a glass of water because your body is dehydrated. The right prescription is going to depend on the nature of the problem.

The same is true when you're trying to optimize an e-commerce website. You want to follow qualitative and quantitative clues to a diagnosis. *Then* prescribe a solution. The user's headache is that they couldn't quickly and easily find boots. A navigational problem may have caused that headache. Or something more systemic and site-wide may have.

How do you find out the real problem? The trick is to, as John

Cutler, Head of Education for Amplitude, says, "think big, work small."[37]

In e-commerce, thinking big means seeing the whole picture. It's understanding how visitors experience a site and what their holistic journey looks like—their joys, pain points, frustrations, expectations, aha moments, and so on.

Working small means favoring contained, iterative improvements (see Chapter 2, "The Scientific Method, Not Silver Bullets").

As Cutler pointed out, great teams and brands do both. Brands who "think big, work big" fall prey to the redesign circle of disaster, where they annually rely on massive redesigns to fix visitor headaches. They also take forever to make changes— what major redesign has ever happened quickly? On the flip side, brands who "think small, work small" are better at getting changes out there. But "they sprint in circles. The work lacks coherence and feels scattershot. There's a perception of progress, but looking back the team sees a lot of disjointed, reactive work."[38] Their changes are rarely meaningful because they've missed the big picture.

---

37 Cutler explains this approach in a 2020 newsletter: https://cutlefish.substack.com/p/tbm-4653-thinking-big-working-small.

38 Part 2 of Cutler's take on thinking big and working small: https://cutlefish.substack.com/p/tbm-452-think-big-work-small-part.

Teams who "think big, work small" avoid the pitfalls of both extremes. They look for trends in their quantitative and qualitative data and extrapolate those trends to the overall visitor experience. This is thinking big. Then they make small improvements to the visitor's experience and learn from each one. These learnings compound, and the team tests smarter each time. This is working small. Think big, work small.

ISN'T IT ABOUT TIME YOU STEPPED OUT OF THE JAR?

Your knowledge of your store is one of your biggest strengths—and one of your biggest weaknesses. But this doesn't mean you're condemned to end up alone, in an empty warehouse, smoking a cigar, and mulling over mistakes. There's a lot you can do to balance out your weakness, step outside your bias, and significantly improve how visitors and customers experience your brand.

And it all starts with getting outside the jar to understand your customers' experiences.

CHAPTER 6

LAW: CUSTOMER EXPERIENCE DRIVES CONVERSIONS, NOT THE OTHER WAY AROUND

Big idea: Customer experience and conversion rate optimization is a one-way street. A great experience drives conversions, but conversions don't drive experience.

Let's say you own and operate an e-commerce business that sells eco-friendly pesticides. You're called, oh, Random Ants of Kindness. You've spent three years building a small base of regional, repeat purchasers, and sales from them have been steady. However, you're struggling to attract new customers to your website and finding it difficult to get those new visitors to complete a purchase. Despite your continued efforts to drive traffic from paid search and social, your conversion rate is still not where you'd like it to be.

Until recently, your unique products were the only option for consumers seeking a truly eco-friendly alternative to harmful pesticides, but you've noticed an increasing number of competitors emerging in your market. They're selling products similar to your own. Even though you offer a superior product and your core customers are satisfied, you consistently receive complaints about the functionality of your site. And you're watching your sales dwindle as more and more customers switch to the competing brands.

This is a story I've seen play out countless times from businesses that neglect customer experience for the sake of conversion rates.

WHAT IS THE CUSTOMER EXPERIENCE?

When most brands think of customer experience (CX), they think of customer support and product packaging. Although these do play a role in how a customer experiences a brand, CX is much bigger than that.

Imagine a great shopping experience.

It's Saturday morning and you're working on a home project. You're close to finishing, but you just ran out of nails. So you zip over to the local hardware store. The facade is clean and welcoming, with a row of healthy ferns and terra-cotta pots stacked out front. When you walk in, an associate pleasantly greets you. They ask how your day is going and if they can help find anything in particular. You mention nails, and they point you to aisle eight. There, the various nails, screws, brackets, and doodads are all clearly organized and labeled (a godsend for a home dabbler like yourself). You quickly locate the finishing nails you need and are delighted to find there's no line at the checkout. On the way out, the same associate holds the door for you and says, "Have a great day!" You're back in your car in less than five minutes and headed home to finish up the project before lunch.

All of those touchpoints (the facade, associate, store organization and wayfinding, product labels, checkout, parking proximity) make up the customer experience in physical retail, and they all translate to e-commerce in one way or another. The "facade" is your home page. The organized and labeled sections of the store are your navigation. The friendly sales associate is your website copy, product pages, help docs, and live chat. And so on.

This means, for both in-person and online, the customer experience isn't any one moment, channel, or team within a brand (though some progressive and well-funded companies do have a dedicated CX team). CX is the overall quality of interaction your customers have with your brand at every single turn.

This includes the way the customers' friends talk about you, how easily the customer can accomplish their goals on your site, whether your brand adds delight or friction to their journey, and every single big or small brand impression along the way—ads, chat, landing pages, purchase confirmation pages, your loyalty program, and more.

To put it succinctly, CX is the sum of every interaction between a customer and your brand, from the first time they hear about you to the most recent touchpoint they've experienced.

And when the customer experience is great, brands experience substantial benefits (further proof, by the way, that your goals and your customers' goals align). Here are just a few benefits of creating a great customer experience:

- Companies with excellent customer experience drive revenues 4 percent to 8 percent higher than competitors.[39]
- Sixty-five percent of consumers say they were more

---

39 "45 Ecommerce Stats for Accelerated Digital Transformation."

strongly influenced by a positive experience than a great ad campaign.[40]

- Eighty-six percent of consumers will pay more for a better customer experience.[41]
- Ninety-two percent of companies improving their customer experience saw an increase in customer loyalty.[42]

As Katelyn Bourgoin, CEO of Customer Camp, put it, if you want to double your monthly recurring revenue, "DOUBLE the time you invest in learning about your customer. Customer experience (CX) is the best growth hack."[43]

Take DTC women's body product subscription service, Billie. From the start, Billie has been laser-focused on who they're serving. They've focused specifically on women who are fed up with paying over 7 percent more for razors while having ten times the surface area of men to shave. "We also set out to build a very different kind of relationship with women," Co-founder Georgina Dooley says, "compared to what other razor companies had done in the past. Instead of speaking to women in clichés and making them

---

40   Tom Puthiyamadam and José Reyes, "Experience Is Everything: Here's How to Get It Right," PWC (2018), https://www.pwc.com/us/en/advisory-services/publications/consumer-intelligence-series/pwc-consumer-intelligence-series-customer-experience.pdf.

41   "2011 Customer Experience Impact Report," Oracle (2011), http://www.oracle.com/us/products/applications/cust-exp-impact-report-epss-1560493.pdf.

42   "Dimension Data 2017 Global CX Benchmarking Report," https://dimensiondatacx.com/?utm_source=Referral&utm_medium=PR-Regional&utm_campaign=GCXBR2017.

43   Bourgoin tweeted this anecdote: https://twitter.com/KateBour/status/920113151651319808.

feel ashamed about their body hair, we wanted to celebrate womankind and reinforce that shaving is a personal choice, not an expectation."[44] This customer understanding and the experience Billie built around it paid off. They achieved their first year's sales goals in just a few months.

Billie isn't an anomaly either. Look at some of the fastest-growing DTC brands—like beauty darling Glossier—and you'll find customer experience sitting at the core of their strategy.

Great Customer Experience Builds a Long-Term Competitive Advantage

These brands know that in addition to boosting revenue, amazing CX builds a difficult-to-breach moat.

Quick history context: in ye olde days, cities and castles had huge ditches around them called moats. (You've no doubt seen these in storybooks or pictures.) Sometimes they were filled with water, usually not. Oftentimes, they were a result of building a big wall or rampart around the city or castle—you created a ditch when you took out a massive load of dirt.

These moats were a great defense against attacks. At a minimum, they slowed down invaders and made them easier

---

44 Georgina Mooley, "How the Founder of Billie Razors Is Disrupting the Male-Dominated Shaving Industry," *Time*, July 12, 2018, https://time.com/5336199/billie-founder-disrupt-shaving-industry/.

targets for city defenders. Moats also limited access points to the city, and fewer access points are easier to defend. What's more, they prevented enemies from creating *new* access points, such as moving towers or ladders, which you had to put against the city wall. (Fun fact: contrary to popular belief, folks never put crocodiles in their moats, but one family in the Czech Republic has had bears in theirs since 1707.[45])

This reliable defense system is where the idea of a business or "economic moat" (popularized by Warren Buffett) comes from. It's when your company has a distinct, defensible advantage over competitors that allows you to protect your market share and profitability.

Creating an airtight consumer experience is one effective way to build a moat around your business, and the better the experience, the wider the moat. Long term, this means when competitors emerge (and they inevitably will, if they haven't already) and attempt to steal your customer base via discounted products or other tactics, you'll retain the upper hand because your website offers a seamless purchasing experience.

---

45 Nowadays, the bears are celebrities: https://castle.ckrumlov.cz/docs/en/zamek_1nadvori_mpriko.xml.

TACTICAL RECOMMENDATION: BUILD A MOAT BEFORE ENTERING NEW MARKETS

As you grow, you may sign on with third-party distributors, like Amazon, to reach more potential customers. When you do this, you are, in a sense, competing against yourself, and there are a few dangers that come with this territory.

The first danger is a sharp drop-off in your store sales. It's important to remember consumers are very familiar with distributors. They know them, trust them, and will often use them even if the price is slightly higher there. This is doubly true if your website is rife with experience issues.

The second danger is driving visitors to competitors. Let's say you sell camping gear, but you provide a poor product page experience (on your site and with the distributor). In particular, you don't offer many benefits, details, or dimensions that help the consumer decide whether your particular gear suits their particular camping needs (Is it ideal for RVs? Car camping? Multiday backpacking?). So visitors hop over to REI, or Reddit, or any number of hiker forums. Once there, they encounter an extensive list of competitor products others have used and tested alongside yours. This plants a pernicious seed of doubt and frequently moves the visitor further away from a purchase—now, they're checking out competitor options and may not return to your product at all.

An excellent customer experience is a good way to ward off both of these dangers. And it's why you want to create an experience moat before you expand. This puts you at a competitive advantage before you go into new markets and helps you maintain strong sales through your e-commerce site, even after launching with distributors.

Granted, much of this information may not be breaking news to you. Customer experience is becoming more of a focal point for DTC brands, and many site owners understand—at least conceptually—that experience matters.

The trouble is, many brands think the relationship between customer experience and conversion rate optimization is a two-way street. This is not the case.

WHERE MOST BRANDS GET CUSTOMER EXPERIENCE AND CONVERSION RATE OPTIMIZATION WRONG

It's hard to find an e-commerce site that doesn't serve up a pop-up as soon as you hit their site. These often say something along the lines of, "Receive x in exchange for your email address." There's a reason for this.

Email is a valuable channel, and these pop-ups do gather email addresses. They achieve a conversion but at the expense of a poor customer experience.

For starters, this experience is a bit like a sales associate jumping in your face as soon as you walk into a store; it's disruptive and annoying. If that happened to you as soon as you walked into a retail store, you'd have a pretty negative reaction. (Remember, just because you can't see the visitor on the other side of the screen doesn't mean you shouldn't treat them as if they just walked into your retail store.)

Also, visitors tend to receive these pop-ups *every time* they land on the site, either because the brand is sloppy with the pop-up implementation, or the visitor is running ad-blockers or has disabled cookies. This means the visitor experiences the pop-up frustration not once but every single time they visit the site.

Some brands realize this and still justify the pop-up. However, they often overlook the fact the pop-up isn't just creating friction for the customer; it's creating friction for the brand as well. Especially if the brand is offering a discount, the same visitor (or returning customer) will enter a different email address multiple times to receive the discount.

This is costly for the brand in terms of revenue as well as data.

Multiple email addresses muddy lifetime value, dilute open rates, and dull email efficacy. You're not only paying to send more emails to more subscribers (who aren't opening the emails because it's their junk email address), but you're also landing in Promotions or Spam and tarnishing your email send name in the eyes of Gmail and other mail providers who pay attention to how folks respond to your emails.

What's more, brands often create bad customers through this process. They gather an email address with a discount, and that consumer will forever be a discount consumer. (See Chapter 8, "Discounting Isn't Optimization: It Is Margin Drain," for more on this.)

So you've collected an email address, yes, but at what cost?

What this illustration shows is that conversion does not always equal a good experience. You can have an activity that achieves (at least temporarily) a lift in conversion rates while also lowering the quality of the experience.

Conversion rate optimization and CX isn't a two-way street; an improvement to one doesn't automatically equal an improvement to the other. In fact, it's very much a one-way street: a healthy customer experience can significantly improve a conversion rate, but a high conversion rate doesn't generate a healthy consumer experience. The relationship flows only one way.

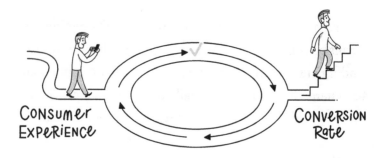

CONSUMER EXPERIENCE

CONVERSION Rate

THREE MISCONCEPTIONS SUSTAINING THE TWO-WAY-STREET MYTH

If this is true, why does the two-way-street myth persist? It's largely thanks to several related CX misconceptions. Here are three big ones.

"We're fine now, so we'll be fine later."

Something I frequently hear from brands is their conversion rate is already in a good place, so they don't need to worry about altering their website experience. This usually sounds like, "Oh, we're already doing a 5 percent conversion rate. How much better can it get?"

However, brands with some level of product-market fit are going to have at least a decent conversion rate. This especially true if they're selling a great product, and there's an immediate need for their customers to purchase it, regardless of how positive or negative the consumer experience is.

And remember latent effects from Chapter 6, "Customer

Experience Drives Conversions, Not the Other Way Around." If your website isn't providing a great experience now, you'll experience pains later, much like our fictional Random Ants of Kindness did. Once their customers had the option to purchase a similar product without having to deal with a poor purchasing experience, they chose the next best alternative. You can bet your customers will, too.

Also, don't forget the best conversion rate is one that's always improving. Regardless of the current rate, the customer experience, and thus the conversion rate, can always be improved.

"Oh, well, most visitors don't even know what they want."

Another objection brands raise is you can't optimize an e-commerce experience for what visitors want because most visitors don't know *what* they want. The brand is there, myth-holders argue, to tell the visitor what they want.

These brands are also fond of an alleged Henry Ford quote: "If I had asked people what they wanted, they would have said faster horses."

There are several issues here. For starters, there's no evidence Ford ever said that (and his inability to respond to customer needs negatively impacted Ford Motor Company).[46] What's more, online visitors *do* know what they want and are often looking for something very specific. They're not on your website to hear your sage-like recommendations; they're on your website to see whether you can solve their pain or need and, if so, how they can buy that solution. Imagine walking into a grocery store for a loaf of bread and the manager tries to steer you toward the cantaloupe!

"The brand brought them to the website."

The third big misconception is the site is about the brand experience, not the customer experience, because the brand brought visitors to the website in the first place.

Although marketing does play a key role in getting visitors to your site and that marketing may include brand messages, once visitors arrive on your site, your marketing is

---

46 There's no evidence tying Ford to this quote, though many folks have looked for it. Patrick Vlaskovits, "Henry Ford, Innovation, and That 'Faster Horse' Quote," *Harvard Business Review*, August 29, 2011, https://hbr.org/2011/08/henry-ford-never-said-the-fast.

done (see Chapter 4, "Once Visitors Arrive, Stop Marketing to Them."

If visitors aren't looking for your company history, there's no reason to push it in front of them. Consumers search for solutions to their needs (which is rarely to hear your brand story, by the way), and search engines are much better at providing resources for what visitors want than your brand's marketing. Once they're on your site, the less friction there is throughout the customer journey, the better.

REALITY CHECK: YOUR CX PROBABLY ISN'T ALL THAT GREAT—AND IT'S DEFINITELY HURTING CONVERSIONS

Your customer experience could almost certainly use improvement. But I don't mean that as a personal attack—it's true of every brand I meet.

Historically, data shows brands think they're doing a much better job than customers think they're doing. A survey by Gladly found 86 percent of companies believe they provide customers with a seamless experience versus only 40 percent of customers who say they experience seamlessness.[47] Separate research from Capgemini found that whereas 75 percent of companies believe they're customer-centric,

47 "45 Ecommerce Stats for Accelerated Digital Transformation."

only 30 percent of customers actually believe it.[48] Even more startling, only 12 percent of people believe a business when they say, "We put the customer first."[49]

There's clearly a gap between the experience brands think they're providing and the experience customers are actually receiving. Actions speak louder than words; the experience you're providing on your website speaks louder than the experience you claim you're providing in your value statements.

Why aren't brands catching this? Part of the reason is, they're stuck inside the jar (see Chapter 5, "You Can't Read the Label from inside the Jar." Another reason is, experience issues aren't as obvious as we imagine.

EXPERIENCE ISN'T AN ALL-AWESOME OR ALL-TERRIBLE DICHOTOMY

Customer experience is multifaceted and involves many touchpoints. For this reason, it's rare any brand has a wholly awful or wholly phenomenal experience. Although

---

48 Mark Taylor, Jerome Buvat, Amol Khadikar, and Yashwardhan Khemka, "The Disconnected Customer: What Digital Customer Experience Leaders Teach Us about Reconnecting with Customers," Capgemini Consulting (2017), https://www.capgemini.com/wp-content/uploads/2017/07/the_disconnected_customer-what_digital_customer_experience_leaders_teach_us_about_reconnecting_with_customers.pdf.

49 Marcus Andrews, "42% of Companies Don't Listen to Their Customers. Yikes," HubSpot, June 11, 2019, https://blog.hubspot.com/service/state-of-service-2019-customer-first.

it's human nature to want to sort overall experiences into Goldilocks-style buckets—too hot, too cold, just right—the truth is, most brands offer a mixed bag of good and bad.

A good experience happens when a customer feels positive about interacting with a brand. You can probably think of no less than ten examples of this offhand. These happen when a frustration turns into a resolution (the service recovery paradox), you find the right content at the right time, checkout meets your expectations, and so on.

A bad experience is when a customer has a poor taste in their mouth (literally or figuratively) after interacting with your brand. These can be as notable as receiving a package in the mail that's so ripped and battered that it clearly endured a game of shipping soccer. Yet, most poor experiences *aren't* this obvious, and that's part of the reason they endure. Think of it this way: if you step on a nail, you'll immediately yelp and fix the problem. But if you're rubbing blisters, you won't notice those for quite some time. The blister pain isn't evident at first. You can walk miles before you notice a few slightly bothersome hotspots and many more miles until seriously uncomfortable blisters develop.

The nail in this analogy is explosively bad e-commerce experiences, and brands are generally quick to fix these. They're obvious and obviously costly. The blisters are the more subtly poor experiences. They don't cause visitors to yelp as nails would, and the immediate impact is less obvious than a hole-shaped wound in their heels. Yet, given enough friction and time, they still make for a miserable experience.

Take product dimensions and sizes. Ideally, these help the customer quickly figure out "is this the one I need?" Most size charts don't do that job very well. For example, an e-commerce store sells a wide selection of bike tires in five sizes. Rather than specifying the dimensions of each tire, they list sizes according to the type of bike the tire usually fits—which requires visitors to navigate a separate size guide that *does* list tire dimensions.

Or let's say you'd like a new yoga mat. You pull up a brand you've heard about and click over to "Mats" in their navigation. The page loads over a hundred mats, and the only way to filter them is by price or popularity. To find the one with the size, materials, and color you want, you'd have to click through tens of products. How many visitors will stick around to do *that*?

These examples may seem small, but any experience that frustrates a visitor or hinders their progress toward their goals (to research or convert) will introduce friction. The more friction you add, the slower the customer progresses (and the slower your conversion flywheel turns). At some point—the point varies per customer—that friction won't be worth the effort. It'll feel like walking through mud or turning into a strong headwind, and your visitors will turn aside.

HOW DO YOU KNOW IF THERE'S FRICTION IN YOUR EXPERIENCE?

How can you tell if you're one of many brands introducing unnecessary friction throughout their visitor's experience? There are at least three ways to spot this in the data you're collecting on your site.

Existing customers fall off to a new competitor

You've seen conversion rates you're fairly happy with until a competitor comes on the scene. Remember, you could provide a somewhat terrible site experience and still have an audience if you offer a necessary product. Customers will stick with you...until there's a better option.

Brand loyalists convert, but new visitors don't

If your website has a relatively low conversion rate of 0.5 percent for new visitors but a relatively high conversion rate of 5 percent for returning visitors, that's a clear symptom of a deeper problem in your consumer experience. Your brand loyalists may continue buying your products because they know and trust your company, but prospective customers who aren't familiar with you will be more hesitant if your website experience is unsatisfactory.

Some disparity here is common. A return visitor's conversion rate is often two to three times higher than a new visitor's conversion rate (this varies some, according to product). But a ten times difference should raise eyebrows.

Your customers tell you there's a gap

If the qualitative feedback you're receiving through social media, newsletter responses, customer support requests, and customer research interviews cite experience issues, you have experience issues.

Keep in mind, spotting these often requires some extrapolation. A visitor will rarely drop you a Twitter thread of the top ten usability issues they encountered on your website. It's more likely you'll hear similar complaints or statements of confusion over and over. For example, a soccer retailer may hear "Do you have any kids' cleats?" (they can't tell from your site), or "I've no idea what size ball my kid needs" (you're not guiding them toward a confident purchase), or "The medium fits more like a small, and the first game is next week" (your sizing chart needs some work). All of these pieces of feedback indicate experience issues.

THE COSTS OF NOT CLOSING THE EXPERIENCE GAP

For the sake of argument, let's say there *is* a big gap between the experience you're offering and the experience you could be offering.

What's the opportunity cost of not closing that gap?

If you're looking at the gap between a bad experience and a good one, the opportunity costs are clear: high churn, poor reviews, few referrals, and low sales. The costs of acquiring new customers are 60 percent higher[50] than five years ago, and 51 percent of consumers say they would churn from a brand after one to two bad experiences.[51] It's extremely difficult to create healthy profit margins if you're losing customers as fast—or faster!—than you can get them.

It's a no-brainer to close a gap this wide. But what if you're looking at the gap between an okay and great experience, or even between a good and great experience? Are those gaps worth closing, too?

Data says yes. XM, a research company focused on experience management, examined feedback from ten thousand US consumers and found customers who have an "okay" experience are 72 percent likely to buy again versus customers who have a "good" experience and are 84 percent likely to purchase again.[52] That's a 12 percent jump between "okay" and "good." And if you bump up a "good" experience to a "very good" experience? A whopping 94 percent are likely to purchase more! (It's worth noting XM reported similar jumps in the customers' likelihood to refer, forgive a poor experience, and trust the brand as well.)

---

50 This is true for both B2B and B2C. Neel Desai, "How Is CAC Changing Over Time?" ProfitWell, August 14, 2019, https://www.profitwell.com/recur/all/how-is-cac-changing-over-time.

51 "45 Ecommerce Stats for Accelerated Digital Transformation."

52 Moira Dorsey, David Segall, and Bruce Temkin, "ROI of Customer Experience, 2020," XM Institute, August 18, 2020, https://www.xminstitute.com/research/2020-roi-cx.

To put this in more tangible terms, let's say you attract 1,000 customers per month. If you have an okay customer experience, 720 of them will buy from you again. But if you have a very good customer experience, 940 of them will buy from you again. What could those 220+ additional purchases you earn every month mean for your business?

There's a good deal of revenue, loyalty, and trust sitting in the gaps between bad, okay, good, and very good experiences. Even if your experience is already "good," it's worth improving it to "very good."

THE 3 WS AND HOW THEY FUEL CONVERSIONS

To improve the customer experience (and fuel conversions), there are a few foundational concepts you'll want to understand and apply. Here are three practices I recommend for ironing out kinks in your experience.

DEFINE WHO IS COMING TO YOUR SITE WITH CUSTOMER PERSONAS

The foundation for a seamless consumer experience on your website is clearly defining your ideal customer personas (the way Billie did). This includes:

- Narrowing down who you serve and who you don't serve (your products aren't for everyone)

- Identifying different types of customers coming to your site
- Gathering basic demographics, e.g., domestic or international
- Expanding basic psychographics: what customers look like, how they act, how they speak, what they're thinking and feeling

Note: If you're still using the same customer personas you created when you launched your website, it's time to think about updating them to reflect your current customers.

Tools that can help you define your customer are customer interviews, surveys, and feedback from your customer service team.

Most brands get this piece wrong by either skipping it altogether or not understanding their customer well enough. The latter mistake occurs when brands do "lazy" customer research and don't build a detailed picture of their customer's needs, pains, and desires (i.e., they stick with a narrow persona such as "Joe is a middle-aged man who likes tools"). More brands do this than you might think. According to an InMoment survey, 74 percent of brands aren't having direct conversations with customers about their experiences.[53]

---

53   "Study: Brands Grossly Overestimate CX Improvements; Blame Customers for Falling Short," InMoment, January 30, 2019, https://inmoment.com/news/study-brands-grossly-overestimate-cx-improvements-blame-customers-for-falling-short/.

And it's rather difficult to understand your customers, let alone personalize an experience for them, if you haven't gotten to know them.

DETERMINE WHY THEY'RE THERE

Earlier in the book, we established visitors are at your site for one of two reasons:

- To research
- Or to convert

This is true but broad. Once you understand who is coming to your site, you can dig into why and uncover more nuance to their goals.

Let's say you sell sneakers. A visitor has arrived to buy some. They're there to convert, yes, but to help them toward their conversion, you need to know why they want to convert. A visitor's why usually boils down to either solving a problem or improving their life—they're either looking for a painkiller or a vitamin.

For our sneaker shopper, this could look like:

- **Painkiller:** The visitor's current pair is worn thin and killing their arches. They want better support and relief from foot pain.

- **Vitamin:** Their wardrobe is missing that perfect pair of white kicks, the kind that goes with everything. They've been envying their friends' and want a pair of their own. Once they have them, they'll feel more cool and confident in their clothes.

Each visitor has different needs, wants, and search processes, even though their overall goal (buy a pair of sneakers) is the same. To help either visitor successfully reach their destination with as little friction as possible, you need to know what's driving them.

Most brands get this piece wrong by focusing on one and only one why. For example, many brands design their experience for cold traffic alone. They fail to provide context—men shop differently than women, self-purchasers shop differently than gift-givers, cold traffic shops differently than referrals.

As Stuart Balcombe, Founder of Discovery Sprints, put it, "Typically, brands start with themselves, with their product, with their business goals, and then they align everything around that. What the customer actually cares about is 'How does this product help me make progress?' and 'Why do I need this product today, not six months ago and not six months from now?'"

To answer those questions, you need to dig into *why* each

type of customer is there and what desires, struggles, and motivations they have as they work toward their goals. Among other things, this is what helps you determine what content to display where, how to structure your site, what to put into product descriptions, what to upsell, and numerous other decisions.

Brands who understand how their product fits into the customer's life as a whole—instead of trying to squeeze the customer into their brand or founder goals—are the ones who get ahead.

TACTICAL TIP: LOOK AT THE PRIMARY SEARCH QUERIES ON YOUR WEBSITE

E-commerce businesses often focus on keywords that bring traffic to their website but neglect the keywords visitors use on their own site. This is a mistake. You want to pay attention to both types of queries.

The keywords and search terms visitors use on your site are a valuable resource that can highlight inefficiencies in your website navigation. For example, if the term "cookware" makes up half of the search queries on your camping store website but isn't clearly listed in the navigation, that's a serious indication of a larger problem with the consumer experience of your site.

FIGURE OUT WHAT IS HOLDING THEM UP

Once you know who is visiting your website and why they're there, you can build out a detailed customer journey map. From an e-commerce perspective, a customer journey map shows how customers interact with your brand from the customer's perspective versus sales and marketing funnels, which are usually from the brand's perspective.

It also integrates data from all your tools and research into a unified view. This gives you the ability to "walk in your customer's shoes" through each stage of their experience with you (from before they hear about you, to exploring your site, to post-purchase, and beyond). The best maps also pinpoint what a visitor feels and wants at each stage, based on interviews and other qualitative feedback.

Overall, this gives you a visual of bottlenecks, roadblocks, and friction points you'd otherwise miss. This, by the way, is one reason eight out of ten CX, analytics, and marketing professionals say a journey-based strategy is critical to a business's success.[54]

---

54 Stephanie Ventura, "2021 Survey: The State of Journey Management & CX Measurement," Pointillist (blog), https://www.pointillist.com/blog/cx-survey-2021-journey-management-cx-measurement/.

HOW OLIPOP PRIORITIZES A
FRICTIONLESS JOURNEY

Some brands view CX as a fire extinguisher—a reactive tool you use to put out fires, de-escalate tense conversations, or smooth over social media mentions. But not OLIPOP, a healthier soda alternative sold in over four thousand stores and online. Eli Weiss, Director of CX at OLIPOP, knows CX is much more powerful than that. He's seen CX function as a powerful acquisition and retention tool, and so he invests a good deal of time getting to know customers and making them feel like friends and family. His team listens, engages, and shares customer data across all teams in the company, and they drive incredible revenue as a result.

Nowhere is this as evident as in OLIPOP's subscriptions. Weiss and his team knew customers were wary of Comcast-like subscriptions—the ones that lock you into convoluted contracts and make canceling so painful that you'd consider hiring someone to do it for you. To combat this subscription stigma, Weiss says, "When customers sign up, we encourage them to skip orders when necessary, and we encourage them to swap flavors."[55] Not only that, but OLIPOP also makes it shockingly easy for customers to do these things.

---

55 Hear Weiss talk about customer support and experience on the *Gorgias* podcast: https://www.gorgias.com/blog/olipop-sms.

So easy, all it takes is a text message. If a subscriber tires of a flavor or simply desires a change, they can text SWAP to OLIPOP. They receive a numbered list of options in return and can send a quick "1" to switch to Strawberry Vanilla or "3" for Orange Squeeze. Roughly 70 percent of subscribers have skipped an order or swapped a flavor, so this meets a clear need in their customers' journey. Weiss says understanding that journey and providing a seamless experience around it has played a big role in their success. He notes, "not putting that big old gate, not telling your customers 'you're stuck in this forever' and just giving that flexibility and removing all kinds of friction" is what has helped OLIPOP grow faster than competing brands.

How fast? In less than ninety days, OLIPOP leaped from under three hundred subscriptions to two thousand.[56] Ninety days later, they doubled it again—almost 35 percent of OLIPOP's business. And because they've carefully guarded their SMS relationship with customers (Weiss notes others look at what they've done and say, "You're barely advertising on it!"), customers listen when they make an announcement. A recent early-access text flavor launch generated $15,000 in sales in less than fifteen minutes—without any discounts.

Product subscriptions or not, strive to be like OLIPOP.

---

56 Weiss shared some of these stats in a Twitter thread: https://twitter.com/eliweisss/status/1318207444435279873.

Once you know who is visiting, why they're there, and what the problems are, it's a matter of prioritizing which ones to fix first.

MAKE A GREAT CUSTOMER EXPERIENCE THE HEARTBEAT OF YOUR SITE

Potential customers who visit your e-commerce website have given you the gift of their attention and the permission to speak to them. It's your job to provide that visitor with a seamless consumer experience, rather than push them through the conversion funnel as quickly as possible.

Directing all of your attention toward improving your conversion rate will only hurt you in the long term. Instead, focus on creating an optimized purchase experience, and your conversion rate will follow suit.

A great consumer experience is the foundation for a great conversion rate, but that correlation works only one way. If you dedicate all of your time and resources toward achieving a higher conversion rate, your consumer experience will suffer, and you'll end up hindering the sustained growth of your business.

Remember, you and your customers both have the same goal: to convert. A good consumer experience is the sustainable path to a good conversion rate.

CHAPTER 7

LAW: IF YOU WANT MORE CONVERSIONS, EARN MORE TRUST

Big idea: Consumers don't trust your store by default. You have to earn that trust on several different levels.

Consumers buy from brands they trust. We know this. But most consumers don't inherently trust the brands they meet. Shiv Singh, the author of *Savvy: Navigating Fake Companies, Fake Leaders and Fake News in a Post-Truth Era*, explains, "Brands do not have the natural, organic credibility that they once did."[57] Trust is no longer the default. What happened?

---

57 Singh elaborates on the post-truth era in an interview with Kate MacArthur, Ipsos: https://future.
   ipsos.com/truth/how-should-brands-protect-their-truth.

A good deal of it has to do with economics and current events. Brands don't operate in a vacuum; they operate in society, and society has been pretty turbulent of late. Richard Edelman, CEO of Edelman global communications, theorizes major violations of the social contract (government corruption, fake news, corporate wrongdoing) have all significantly damaged public trust. The result is rampant fear, even when the economy is improving. After conducting their annual 2021 trust survey, Edelman writes, "Fears are stifling hope, as long-held assumptions about the benefits of hard work and citizenship have been upended...Three in four [respondents] are worried that fake news will be used as a weapon. Six in ten fear the pace of technological change; they are no longer in control of their destiny."[58]

And although businesses currently hold more public trust than either government or nonprofits—they're the only type of organization the public thinks can be both competent and ethical—they're still on shaky ground. In that trust survey, 56 percent of respondents agreed that business leaders are purposely trying to mislead people by gross exaggerations or false claims.[59]

---

58 Richard Edelman, "The Evolution of Trust" (research), Edelman (2020), https://www.edelman.com/research/evolution-trust.

59 Via Edelman's 2021 Trust Barometer report: https://www.edelman.com/sites/g/files/aatuss191/files/2021-01/2021-edelman-trust-barometer.pdf.

To boil it down, consumers may be more *likely* to trust businesses than other organizations, but that trust still has to be earned. It isn't the default.

This should concern e-commerce brands. You *have* to establish credibility and trust with your audience to optimize conversion rates and increase sales. Your visitors need to know they're in the right place, buying from the right people. They also need to verify their conclusion by confirming others feel the same way about your brand. On top of that, many visitors also need to know you're improving the world they live in.

That's a tall order. How do you meet it?

SHOW WHEN YOU CAN; TELL WHEN YOU CAN'T

Building trust through your website is all about what you do. The adage "Actions speak louder than words" comes to mind here, and it applies to brands as much as it applies to our interpersonal relationships.

I realize this borders on sounding trite—"just, you know, show them they can trust you!" And there's a reason I'm not ending this chapter here. Building trust isn't as simple as it sounds. In truth, each touchpoint in the customer journey is an opportunity to build trust—or break it. From the moment a visitor first lands on your site, to the thank-you page they're shown post-purchase, to the emails you send loyal customers, all of these are opportunities.

And from our observation, consumers evaluate trust based on three questions:

1. "Is this a legit store?"
2. "What do others think of it?"
3. "Do I feel good about giving them my personal and payment information?"

And the three buckets of criteria visitors use to answer those questions:

1. Performance, usability, and design
2. Social proof
3. Brand integrity and social impact

A few notes on these questions and criteria before I look at each one.

- First, the overall theme you'll see in each of these is understanding your customers and catering to their needs. If you do that well at every touchpoint, you'll effectively build trust and nurture conversions.
- Second, many of these buckets overlap. For comprehension, I've separated them into neat piles, but keep in mind they're all interconnected.

- Third, trust isn't an either-or thing. It's not something you definitely have or definitely don't. Much like our interpersonal relationships, our trust in brands is built (and lost) incrementally. That's why nurturing it throughout the entire journey—and not just here and there—is so vital.

"IS THIS A LEGIT PLACE?"

One of the first questions first-time visitors will ask is, "Is this a legit website?" What they're assessing here is credibility, and they'll quickly decide that within the first few seconds of landing on your home page. Their evaluation criteria are primarily performance, usability, and design.

PERFORMANCE

Initially, their decision focuses on functionality. This often comes down to load times and bugginess. If the visitor has to wait longer than a few seconds for your site to load or encounters a grievous technical bug up front (e.g., all the text overlaps), most will bounce without ever exploring your products, let alone completing a purchase. From a consumer's perspective, this quick dismissal makes sense: "If you can't fix your website, how can I trust you with my money?"

USABILITY

But let's say you pass the quick technical test. The next thing visitors evaluate is ease of operation—as in, can they find what they are looking for? And really, the heart of this question is, "Does this brand care about me?"

This is not unlike how we evaluate the trustworthiness of someone we've just met. Most of us (consciously or unconsciously) look for empathy cues when we meet someone new. Does the person listen to you or talk at you? Do they ask you questions about yourself or go on and on about things you don't care about? Do they thoughtfully respond to comments you make or simply wait for you to finish so they can start their own commentary? If the other person appears to give a damn about us, we're more likely to trust them. If they don't, the relationship falters before it even begins.

Likewise, consumers are looking for similar empathy cues when they visit your site. It happens quickly, and again, it's not often a conscious process, but it happens nonetheless. The cues consumers look for include intuitive navigation, relevant and consistent content, compelling value propositions, ease of operation, and other factors that indicate "this brand cares about me and what I need."

USABILITY TRUST BREAKERS:
BEWARE OF DARK PATTERNS

The term "dark patterns" was coined by Harry Brignull in 2010 to describe deceptive user interfaces in apps and websites.[60] These interfaces are intentionally designed to trick or manipulate users into doing something they don't want to do.

Imagine two buttons side by side, one green and one red. The green button says, "No" and the red button says, "Yes." You're more likely to click "No" because it's green, a color normally associated with "Yes."

Dark patterns like these "work" in the sense they achieve a specific conversion but at a cost that doesn't justify the means. It's a bit like a mean prank. A mean prank "works" in the sense that it may get a laugh from the crowd or embarrass a friend, but the cost is a damaged relationship. (The worse the prank, the worse the damage.) Likewise, when consumers feel like they've been tricked or manipulated, you damage their relationship with your brand. As a result, your customer lifetime value will fall and there's a good chance those upset customers will tell their friends about their negative experience.

Here are some trust-breaching dark patterns to avoid:

---

60 Brignull explores all things dark patterns at https://www.darkpatterns.org/. Check out the "Hall of Shame" for examples.

- **Confirm shaming** uses shame to prompt action. Many e-commerce websites use pop-ups where the opt-out option is worded so that the user feels guilty or foolish if they don't comply.

- **Bait and switch** promotes a product or service as either totally free or drastically reduced in price. However, when people try to get the product, they discover it's unavailable or only available in very small quantities. Customers are then given the option of buying something that costs more or is of lesser quality.

- **Auto-opt** automatically checks a Yes box for email and product subscriptions. It signs the customer up for either (or both) by default.

- **Forced continuity** is when a consumer isn't given the opportunity or reminded to opt out of a trial. Instead, they're billed automatically when the trial expires. Brands often couple this dark pattern with the one below.

- **Roach motel** is when it's easy for a user to get into a situation but very difficult for them to get out of it. Often, there are negative consequences for backing out, which makes users less inclined to do it. Impossible-to-cancel subscriptions are a prime example of this.

- **Hidden costs**, such as taxes or delivery fees at checkout. (Fact: 56 percent of consumers will abandon their cart if they're presented with unforeseen charges and fees at checkout.[61])

---

61   Stephanie Chevalier, 2021. "U.S. Shopping Cart Abandonment Rates of Selected Categories 2018" Statista, July 7, 2021, https://www.statista.com/statistics/232285/most-common-products-services-abandoned-digital-carts-internet-users/.

- **Sneak into basket** is similar to hidden costs but worse. It's when a site automatically adds products into shoppers' carts (e.g., insurance or add-ons), forcing them to manually remove these items if the purchaser doesn't want them.
- **Price comparison prevention** is where visitors are prevented from comparing prices between different products or services. The thinking is, if customers can't see the prices, they'll buy brand-preferred items (such as those with the highest profit margins). The reality is, this practice leaves customers frustrated and drives them to shop elsewhere.

More than any other criteria, usability is an opportunity to show first-time visitors and customers you understand them, empathize with their needs, and are there to help.

Visual Design Another initial factor visitors consider is your visual design. When I say "design" here, I strictly mean visual design, such as imagery and palette, not related components such as user experience (UX).

Visual design matters, but not as much as most brands think it does. Although e-commerce brands often spend a great deal of time and money on here, I've found (through user testing and work with clients) that the visual design of a site actually matters very little to consumers. Even though a brand believes they need to have a 9/10 or 10/10 design to convert a visitor, in reality, they need only a 4/10 or 5/10 to display enough trust for a visitor to convert.

Put another way, it's more of a trust qualifier than a trust guarantee. Visual design can help you keep a visitor around so you can build trust with them through usability factors and proof, but it's not the one thing that marks you as trustworthy. Think of visual design as the human equivalent of looking friendly or kind. If someone looks "nice" (and that often requires as little as a genuine smile), we're more *likely* to trust them, but few of us automatically grant pretty or nice-looking folks our full trust. After all, every one of us has met outwardly beautiful and inwardly malicious people. Likewise, a pleasing visual design will help you start building trust, but it's not going to do all the trust legwork for you.

With that in mind, there are a few key trust-building areas you'll want to pay attention to in your visual design.

1. Footers

Users go to the footer for three key reasons—jobs, trust signifiers, and last-ditch navigation when they are lost. Although these are often an afterthought, they can have a notable impact on conversions. For example, an A/B test of a luxury handbag website increased sales conversions over 23 percent and increased revenue per visitor by nearly 16 percent—all through a simple redesign of the website footer.[62]

---

62 Expert commentator, "How Does Your Website Footer Impact Conversion?" Smart Insights, December 4, 2012, https://www.smartinsights.com/conversion-optimisation/ab-multivariate-testing/how-does-your-website-footer-impact-conversion/.

Build trust here by posting the name of your business and your contact information clearly and making it easy to locate. Based on our decade-plus of testing, one of the main ways folks initially tell if a site is legit is they scroll right down to the footer and look in the bottom-right corner for (1) an address, (2) a phone number, (3) an email address, and (4) social logos.

If those four things are there, the trust factor goes way up.

Prospects want to know you are real, and real companies have physical addresses and phone numbers, not just email addresses.

2. Imagery

Getting imagery right boils down to quality and relevance. Quality-wise, make sure you use high-quality images that aren't pixelated (even at large screen sizes—check this!). And if you must use stock photos, make sure you craft a cohesive visual aesthetic. A calming Norwegian vibe on the home page followed by an energetic neon downtown vibe on the product category page will jar your visitor.

Likewise, you want to ensure the overall feel of your site appeals to your primary customer base. We've seen companies hire designers who have great ideas but poor knowledge of the audience. The results are invariably disastrous. You'll see few cowboys buying their jeans at Bergdorf Goodman. And you'll see few socialites purchasing a dress at Wilco Farm Store. Keep your imagery relevant to the audience your brand serves.

Also, show photos of your people. Don't stop at headshots of your CEO and officers; show behind-the-scenes shots of your customer service people helping solve problems, your production line getting orders ready, and your developers working on the latest challenge. Remember, people like to do business with people, not with brands. The more personal you are, the more opportunity you have for building trust and confidence.

3. Language and terminology

The third area of visual design you'll want to pay attention to is your copy. Use the same words on your site that your primary audience uses to describe your products and services (i.e., the words they use in their reviews and on social media). Use industry-speak only where your customer would do the same. Shoppers trust language they understand, and they don't want to have to consult a dictionary to understand your descriptions or offers.

Finally, proofread your copy for grammar and spelling. If you can't spell a common word correctly, how can shoppers trust you to get the order right? I've even seen educational sites with misspelled words, and that's a prime example of a confidence sinkhole. The more capable you are of getting the simple things right, the more your visitors will believe you can get the bigger things right.

Once you've established credibility, the next question they ask is, "Well, what do others think about them?"

"DO OTHER PEOPLE TRUST THIS PLACE?"

Imagine you're looking for a general contractor who can do some renovations on your home. You have three contenders. All say they're trustworthy and, so far, all *appear* to be trustworthy: they've listened to your vision, quickly delivered an estimate, and quoted comparable prices. But you're still wary. You've been burned in the past, and you know each of these contractors have an agenda—to smooth-talk their way to your wallet.

So to make your decision, you look up reviews. One contractor has zero reviews. Another has five mixed reviews, and the third has over one hundred and they're mostly positive. Which one would *you* choose?

I bet nearly every reader will choose the one with a hundred reviews. It's human nature to avoid mistakes. We hate looking foolish, and we've all been tricked enough to fear having the wool pulled over our eyes. We don't want to guess we're making a good decision—we want to *know*. And to build confidence, we look to peers. Peers don't have agendas (at least, not ones we usually know of), and so we believe what our peers say quicker than we accept claims made by sales copy or salesmen. It's the easiest way for us to assess whether the assertions the brand is making are truly accurate.

How effective is social proof at driving business for e-commerce businesses? Glossier is a good example of a brand that's done this well. CEO Emily Weiss says, "Eighty percent of Glossier's growth and sales come through peer-to-peer recommendations or our own channels."[63]

There are several ways brands can lean into this reality and demonstrate the various ways others trust the brand. The following are all forms of social trust-builders, signals that say, "Hey, other people think we're great, too—you're in good company if you choose us."

REVIEWS FROM PURCHASERS

Customer reviews are the number one source for visitors trying to decide whether a brand is trustworthy. Nearly 95 percent of shoppers read online reviews before making a

---

63   Amy Farley, "A Breakout Branding Master Class from Glossier, Sweetgreen, Away, and Walker & Co.," *Fast Company*, January 12, 2018, https://www.fastcompany. com/40509036/a-breakout-branding-master-class-from-glossier-sweetgreen-away-and-walker-co.

purchase, and the purchase probability for a product with five reviews is 270 percent greater than the purchase probability of a product with none.[64]

Having reviews matters, but so does the variety, accuracy, legitimacy, and relevancy of your reviews. For one, you want to make sure your reviews all come from verified purchasers (i.e., don't have an open submission form for reviews on a product detail page). And you always want to keep bad reviews around. Many brands' first reaction to negative reviews is to remove them, but this is a mistake. A better approach is to respond to them. Products and websites with all five-star reviews tend to appear dishonest and treacherous to consumers—they feel "off" to us in the same way a too-perfect person feels "off."

On top of that, don't be afraid to get creative with how you're collecting and highlighting reviews on your website. Medelita, an apparel company for healthcare workers, is a great example. When they collect reviews, they ask what role the reviewer is in. For example, whether they're an MD (doctor of medicine) or RN (registered nurse). The specific needs of these roles are different, so it helps visitors to know whether the reviewer has a daily job like theirs.

---

64 Via Spiegel Research Center: https://spiegel.medill.northwestern.edu/
how-online-reviews-influence-sales/.

CUSTOMER TESTIMONIALS

Testimonials differ from product reviews in the way they are presented. Testimonials are concise recommendations placed in callout format. Think of reviews as the backbone of social proof and testimonials as the face. Mixing in video testimonials with your written testimonials is a particularly powerful tactic.

CELEBRITY AND INFLUENCER ENDORSEMENTS

Eighty-nine percent of marketers say ROI from influencer marketing is comparable to or better than other marketing channels.[65] The key thing to understand with endorsements is that it doesn't matter how popular or famous the influencer you enlist is, so long as you find someone with an engaged following and credible track record with that following. "Someone could have a million followers and their posts will definitely drive traffic to your site, but that traffic will be mostly irrelevant," Griffin Thall, the Co-founder of Pura Vida bracelets, pointed out. "When you go for someone with a smaller following but a super relevant aesthetic and vibe, their followers are likely to be more active, engaged, and interested in your products."[66]

---

65   Via an annual influencer marketing survey by Mediakix: https://mediakix.com/influencer-marketing-resources/influencer-marketing-industry-statistics-survey-benchmarks/#:~:text=Nearly%20half%20(48%25)%20of,improve%20their%20returns%20in%20 2019.

66   Griffin Thall, "Making Friends with Influencers," yotpo (n.d.), https://www.yotpo.com/direct-to-consumer-ecommerce-marketing/chapter-3/influencer-marketing/.

EXPERT APPROVALS

A stamp of approval from an expert or thought leader in your industry can carry a lot of weight. It reinforces the quality of your product/service and is especially impactful if you're selling products that customers will typically research before purchasing (think mattresses, footwear, and supplements).

A classic example of expert approvals is the skincare industry. Many leading skincare brands lean on the "dermatologist recommended" statement to sell products, and it's worked. A more creative example is Form Nutrition and the value and advice they offer from PhDs in their emails to subscribers. "We founded Form with a desire to pay respect to the complex science that nutrition is and make it understandable," Form Founder Damian Soong said in an email interview. "Expert content is the way we do this; it provides value to users while at the same time establishing trust and authority. People are much more receptive to this kind of relationship than the usual one-way sales traffic."

One thing to keep in mind, though: this kind of trust signal is only effective when the expert is in their lane. Don't claim a doctor of literature approves a vitamin, for example.

Depending on your client list and product type, displaying your client logos may also serve as a form of expert approval. For example, say a service offers text messaging capabilities for e-commerce companies. If you see a brand like Patagonia uses it, this indicates that experts in the e-commerce space approve of your product. Likewise, if visitors see a renowned brand in their space uses you, they'll interpret this as a type of expert approval.

EARNED MEDIA AND PRESS

Trust in media outlets is declining, but if consumers see you've been published in a reputable one, this still carries a positive impression. So don't hesitate to show logos and lists of news organizations who've written about you—as long as it's a genuine endorsement. (Paying for an ad in a magazine and saying you "appeared in it" doesn't constitute an endorsement, and consumers are getting wise to this tactic.)

USER-GENERATED CONTENT

User-generated content can be anything from photos of customers wearing your brand (see Madewell, Warby Parker, and Glossier), to recipes they submit, to beauty tips they've shared. This form of content shows the visitor others buy and trust your brand, use your products, and like them enough to mention it publicly.

FOLLOWER OR ADOPTION COUNT

Your follower or adoption count is also a trust token. A large follower count on Twitter, Instagram, TikTok, or other platforms can signal, "Hey, a lot of people think this brand is worth paying attention to."

An even more powerful variation of this is listing adoption on your site. For example, Quip toothbrushes' home page boasts "over 5 million mouths and counting" with a plethora of customer reviews below the claim.

CERTIFICATION AND TRUST BADGES

Finally, there are certification and trust badges, particularly those related to security. One of the highest contributors to e-commerce cart abandonment is payment security concerns. According to Baymard, 17 percent of shoppers abandon carts because they don't trust sites with their payment information.[67] If your visitors don't completely trust their personal information is safe with your company, they won't buy from you. When used in checkout, we've consistently found that trust badges can elevate the perceived credibility of a website and, in turn, have a positive impact on conversion rates.

---

67 See Baymard Institute's compiled statistics on cart abandonment: https://baymard.com/lists/cart-abandonment-rate.

HOW THE SHOE MART INCREASED
CONVERSIONS WITH BADGES

The Shoe Mart, a high-end footwear brand, approached The Good with the goal of reducing cart abandonment on their website. And they didn't want to utilize discounting or detract from the user experience to do it. To achieve their goal, the team implemented a variety of trust badges (via TrustedSite certification badges) throughout The Shoe Mart's site to establish credibility in each step of the customer journey. Adding these badges on the home page, footer, and checkout page contributed to a 14 percent increase in e-commerce conversion rate for users who were shown the trust marks.

It is possible to go overboard with security logos, though. Keep in mind, these are less about technical security and more about perceived security. If you include too many badges, it looks like overkill. You'll inject doubt into the visitor's mind and reduce trust. A good rule of thumb is only to include trust badges during relevant stages of the customer journey. For instance, emphasize a payment security badge on the checkout page, not next to the price on every product detail page.

Some visitors may convert quickly once they feel you're credible and realize others think you're credible, too. But for many e-commerce brands, there's one other trust hurdle. That hurdle is, "Do I trust my money is doing some good in the world?"

"DO I FEEL GOOD ABOUT GIVING THEM MY MONEY?"

Consumers increasingly want to see companies make a meaningful impact on society. According to Edelman's 2021 trust survey, 68 percent of respondents believe CEOs should step in when the government does not fix societal problems.[68] A much larger study by Axios (they surveyed thirty-four thousand Americans) found 72 percent of respondents said they trusted companies more than the federal government when it came to finding solutions to social issues.[69] In the same survey, 79 percent of respondents said a company's vision of the world is more important now than ever before.

This data indicates that for many consumers, conversions don't simply ride on whether a product and its delivery are trustworthy (though that matters). It also rides on whether the company is trustworthy with the consumer's purchase money beyond a secure transaction—are those dollars also

---

68 See Edelman's 2021 Trust Barometer report: https://www.edelman.com/sites/g/files/aatuss191/files/2021-01/2021-edelman-trust-barometer.pdf.

69 Via research by Axios and The Harris Poll: https://theharrispoll.com/wp-content/uploads/2020/07/HP-RQ-2020-v9.pdf.

improving employees' lives? What about the environment, society, or the global economy?

When a potential purchaser is assessing big questions like these, there are two trust builders they heavily weigh: brand integrity and corporate social responsibility.

BRAND INTEGRITY

Brand integrity is how consumers perceive you. It's influenced by your site, products, product presentation, service, and overall reputation (think word of mouth and media) and pretty much everything else I've covered so far in this chapter. Much like we'll put more trust in a high-integrity individual, consumers put more trust in high-integrity brands. Brands such as Publix, General Mills, Wegmans, and Hershey[70] all enjoy some of the highest reputations among big brand names in the United States.

The most common ways I see brands *diminish* their integrity are outlandish claims and false product guarantees. Outlandish claims are statements such as "The very best quality money can buy!" or "Absolutely unbreakable!" These vague descriptions may sound nice to novice copywriters, but they reek of infomercials to consumers. You want to be real, not ridiculous. If your new line of fishing

---

70   Via research by Axios and The Harris Poll: https://theharrispoll.com/wp-content/uploads/2020/07/HP-RQ-2020-v9.pdf.

rods has been tested and proven "one hundred times stronger than carbon fiber," that's a fact you want to highlight. But don't jeopardize your credibility by claiming the rods are "unbreakable."

You also want to keep a close eye on any binding guarantees you offer (e.g., any "satisfaction guaranteed" promises). These are a powerful way to encourage consumers to purchase. Take Casper's one-hundred-night risk-free trial when you purchase any of their mattresses. It's a good example of a believable guarantee that encourages consumers to buy a mattress online, which is something they may never have done before. But if your guarantees are too outlandish ("The best night of sleep you've ever had!!")—or worse, you don't follow through on your guarantee—you'll lose the consumer's trust and harm your integrity.

CORPORATE SOCIAL RESPONSIBILITY

A factor related to brand integrity is corporate social responsibility (CSR). A business practicing CSR aims to improve society or the environment in the normal course of business. They want their activities to have a net positive impact as opposed to a neutral or net negative impact.

Some brands codify their approach to CSR through a B Corp certification (this is what The Good has), which legally requires companies to consider their impact on employees, customers, suppliers, community, and the environment and be held accountable by a third party. Or 1 percent for the planet, a commitment to donating the equivalent of 1 percent of gross sales directly to environmental nonprofits. But these aren't the only options.

Examples of brands demonstrating CSR in other ways include Thinx and their commitment to improving access to puberty education, Credo's initiative to source clean (safe, organic, and sustainably produced) beauty products, and Unilever's commitment to cutting its use of virgin plastics in half by 2025.[71] These companies all believe they must make a positive impact through their business operations and are taking steps to create that impact. This aligns with consumer expectations that businesses should improve society, and that alignment fosters trust and gives the consumer confidence in converting.

To demonstrate your impact, you can include any badges (e.g., B Corp) on your site or list proof in numbers. Proof in numbers is a bit like social proof but applied to impact. It's where you list how many people you've helped, what percentage of purchases go to certain causes, or how many gallons of water you've helped purify. For example, several proof in number claims Patagonia makes include "68 percent of our line uses recycled materials" and "66,000

---

71   Unilever announced this in a 2019 press release: https://www.unilever.com/news/press-releases/2019/unilever-announces-ambitious-new-commitments-for-a-waste-free-world.html.

workers are supported by Patagonia's participation in the
Fair Trade Program."

WARNING: YOU MUST WALK THE WALK

It's not enough to pay lip service to brand integrity or social causes. If you speak loudly but fail to take action, you'll fall on a double-edged sword. You'll drive away consumers who don't agree with your stance *and* consumers who agree with your stance but won't tolerate inaction.

To make this more concrete, if you vocally support Black Lives Matter in your newsletter, website banners, and on social media, consumers expect you'll carry that support through your board makeup (are any members Black?), employees (do you have equitable hiring practices?), and your product lines (do you support Black-owned suppliers and partners?). For an example of one company walking the walk, check out Ulta. They're working on doubling the number of Black-owned brands it stocks by the end of 2021, plus investing $2 million in quarterly, mandatory training sessions.

These days, you can't expect consumers to give you their trust. You have to earn it by confirming you're credible, trusted by others, and positively impacting their world. Do that, and you'll see a substantial lift in conversions.

CHAPTER 8

LAW: DISCOUNTING ISN'T OPTIMIZATION; IT IS MARGIN DRAIN

Big idea: Discounting isn't conversion rate optimization. When you default to discounts, you damage your brand, customers, and profits. There are alternatives.

Several e-commerce brands notoriously avoid discounts. If you've been eyeing some Mack Weldon pants, don't hold your breath for a 50 percent off clearance event. Likewise, if you're in the market for those new Allbirds shoes or a frosty RTIC cooler for your summer adventures. These brands rarely, if ever, run discounts.

But is that because not discounting is a new, trendy

e-commerce tactic? Much like when high-end coffee shops first broke onto the scene, are these brands simply "too cool" to play like their counterparts ("We, uh, don't *do* Frappuccinos here")?

Or do some of DTC's favorite high-equity brands steer clear of frequent discounts for much more compelling reasons?

Research, psychology, and my own experiences with e-commerce brands all say they're onto something.

WHY MANY BRANDS OFFER DISCOUNTS IN THE FIRST PLACE

Running a business is hard, and running an e-commerce business is no exception. There are plenty of factors that pressure every owner or manager to slash their prices. Here are six of the more common ones.

OVERBUYING AND RELATED INVENTORY ISSUES

Most retailers face this issue regularly. And too much stock could have root causes that range from overbuying, to a poor understanding of customer needs, to bad collaborations (remember those Cole Haan x Slack sneakers?). The common result is, you have piles of unsold product, and you need to steeply cut prices to get rid of them.

MAJOR ECONOMIC OR INDUSTRY SHIFTS

Clothing retailer La Ligne rarely offers discounts outside of two annual sales (Cyber Monday and a sample sale) each year. But when the pandemic hit, this mindset went right out the window. La Ligne's founder Molly Howard told Glossy, "We went from worrying about margins to worrying only about cash flow."[72] To survive, Howard brought their normally in-store sample sale online, expanded its duration, and added fifty additional styles to the sale. Although the pandemic is a unique event, other large economic or industry shifts can cause similar cash flow concern shifts for e-commerce stores.

NEW BRAND WITH LITTLE-TO-NO CLOUT

A new brand with no established reputation and no word-of-mouth clout may discount to build an initial customer base. After all, consumers don't know the new brand and have little reason to trust them. So they use price as a lever to encourage customers to use the product.

CUSTOMER RELATIONSHIP DEFICITS

"DTC brands have built their value proposition on the fact that they're able to build a more direct relationship with

---

72   Danny Parisi, "Inside DTC Brands' Approach to First-Time Discounting," Glossy, April 7, 2020, https://www.glossy.co/fashion/how-dtc-companies-are-aiming-to-discount-without-diluting-the-brand.

their customers," Anna Hensel for Modern Retail notes. "And in order to communicate directly with customers, these brands need a piece of contact information."[73] To get that contact information, many DTC brands dangle the bait of discounts, hoping a small price cut will earn them a foot in the door with potential customers.

PRESSURE TO KEEP UP WITH THE AMAZONS AND WALMARTS

Especially around notable sales holidays, small brands feel the stifling shadow of Amazon, big-box stores, and well-established brands (e.g., Gap) looming over them. These behemoths historically offer big discounts because their big margins allow them to. And those big discounts attract big crowds. To compete for both sales and attention, many small e-commerce stores feel they have to offer big discounts as well.

THE FRENCH FRIES PROBLEM

Yet, there's another reason discounting is a go-to strategy for brands, and it's the most cringeworthy one I see.

The fact is, the sixth reason discounting is all over many e-commerce stores is because it's the easy button, not

---

73   Anna Hensel, "Without First-Time Customer Discounts, DTC Brands Try to Find New Ways to Collect Emails," Modern Retail, October 8, 2019, https://www.modernretail.co/startups/without-first-time-customer-discounts-dtc-brands-try-to-find-new-ways-to-collect-emails/.

because it's the best way to convert customers. Think of discounts as reaching for fast food every time you're hungry. Over 35 percent of Americans (roughly eighty-five million[74]) do this on any given day. Yet, you don't have to be a nutrition expert to know regular fast food is bad for you. Yes, it's convenient, effective (it curbs your hunger), and tastes good. But all these "perks" are deceiving. While you're checking off your short-term needs, you're damaging your long-term health. Worse, if fast food becomes a habit, that habit will put you in a bad spot and corner of the doctor's office down the road.

Discounts are the large fries equivalent for your business.

They're convenient. You can have them up and running in hours, if not minutes. They're effective. They often drive a short-term boost in conversion rate and sales. And they're enjoyable. Who doesn't *like* seeing a spike on their revenue chart?

But once you start on them, they're a hard habit to break. And like those fries, they're seriously damaging to your business's long-term health.

THE SHADOW SIDE OF DISCOUNTING

What kind of long-term impacts are we talking about? Some pretty serious ones.

---

74   Based on consumption data between 2013 and 2016: https://www.cdc.gov/nchs/products/databriefs/db322.htm.

It's important to note the pains I'll cover next aren't surface level. They're not like the headache you get from staring at a computer screen all day—they can't be fixed with an Advil, a glass of wine, and a good book.

Rather, they're pernicious pains. They start imperceptibly, but they grow into something that devastates your brand. They're like the herniated disk (think headache times one hundred) you get from months of poor posture at your desk—insidious, painful, and expensive. They're also widespread: they impact your customers, your reputation, and your financial health.

FINANCIAL IMPACT: MARGIN DRAIN

When you discount, you bring in less profit compared to other incentives such as a free gift with purchase or free shipping over a certain threshold (more on that data in a minute). This is especially damaging to small-margin e-commerce brands, but it's something even bigger retailers aren't immune to. For example, when Macy's had to employ heavy markdowns to clear unsold merchandise in spring 2019, shares dropped 13 percent.[75]

---

75 Lauren Thomas and Courtney Reagan, "Macy's Shares Tank 13% as Deep Discounting Leads to a Big Earnings Miss and a Cut in Forecast," CNBC, August 14, 2019, https://www.cnbc.com/2019/08/14/macys-reports-fiscal-q2-2019-earnings.html.

REPUTATION IMPACT: DILUTED BRAND EQUITY

In Chapter 9, "Your Competition Is a Distraction," I mentioned brand equity is one way brands establish trust with consumers. That equity, aka the value of your brand, is influenced by several factors, including your pricing and advertising.

If you're running frequent discounts, you're training customers to see you as a discount brand. Psychologically, this is a form of classical conditioning, where you repeatedly pair two stimuli together. In this case, the stimuli are your brand and discounts. The long-term result of putting those side by side, over and over, is customers associate your brand with price cuts (the more often you offer discounts, the stronger this perception). This positions you as a coupon brand, and it's very difficult to change this perception.

As Web Smith of DTC industry newsletter 2PM pointed out, "Brands with low equity tend to maintain substantial discounts, year-round. Look no further than J. Crew or Gap for this phenomenon. There isn't a time of year when a casual customer can pay full price."[76]

Think about it. When was the last time you paid full price at Michaels, Kohl's, or Bed Bath & Beyond?

---

76 Via a 2PM member brief: https://2pml.com/2018/11/28/member-brief-bfcm-brand-equity-study/.

STRATEGIC IMPACT: UNHEALTHY FOCUS ON COMPETITORS

When you compete on price, you enter your brand in a race to the bottom. Keep in mind, if price cuts are the easiest thing for you to implement, they are also the easiest thing for your competitors to match. You do 10 percent; competitors do 15 percent. You do 20 percent; they do 25 percent. Although you and your competitor might both win a pricing battle here and there, you'll both lose the discount war over time.

Friendly reminder: other brands are discounting, but that doesn't mean you have to copy them. You have no idea how that tactic is working out for them behind the scenes. They may have higher top-line revenue, but there's a good chance their profitability isn't in tip-top shape—and the company with a better profit margin almost always wins.

DATA IMPACT: POOR EMAIL METRICS

According to research by DMA and Pure360, 23 percent of email users have additional email addresses they use to receive some or all marketing messages. Oftentimes, one of those email addresses is a "trash" email address the consumer never checks.

This is a key problem with baiting consumers for their email address—when they're handing it over for a one-off incentive, you're not guaranteed you'll get the email address they regularly check. On a related note, many consumers use those multiple email addresses to receive the same discount multiple times. A handful of savvy shoppers even know they can create endless emails with their Gmail accounts. For example, if my email is jon@gmail.com (sadly, it's not), then I can enter j.on@gmail.com or jon+1@gmail.com or jon+hello@gmail.com every time I hit a site's home page. And it'll count as a new email address every time.

What this means for brands is additional margin drain, muddied email metrics, and higher email costs to send the same email to the same customer multiple times. Not to mention damage to your sender address when all those emails wind up in promotions or spam.

So although brands throw up discounts and email collection forms thinking they're panning for gold, what they end up catching is fool's gold, and they damage one of their most valuable channels in the process.

HIRING A BUCKET WHEN YOU NEED A PLUMBER

In almost every case, discounting is the result of a problem-solution mismatch. Brands see a leak in their revenue, acquisition, or conversion funnels (problem), and they grab a bucket to fix it (solution mismatch).

Yet, if you're losing customers because of poor traffic quality, bad copywriting, confusing site structure, lack of social proof, or poor customer understanding, well, a discount won't fix those problems. It might help you catch some dripping dollars, but it won't patch the root cause, which is a broken pipe. Discounts can't fix poor pricing strategies, products, or customer fit.

A bucket can't plug holes in the sales funnel.

CAVEAT: THERE ARE TWO INSTANCES WHERE DISCOUNTING MAKES GOOD SENSE

For brands who actually have great plumbing—strong sales, effective conversion funnels, and flourishing customer relationships—a once- or twice-a-year discount can be a smart play. This is why you'll see even brands who are notoriously against discounts offer one here and there.

Bare Performance Nutrition, for example, runs only two sales a year. The founder, Nick Bare, explains, "We pride ourselves on not being a huge discount brand and only run two sales each year—Black Friday and Fourth of July (each being 20 percent off site-wide)."[77] Fun fact: Bare is a veteran, so the July sale is tied directly to his brand's origins.

---

77 Hear more from Bare in a *Starter Story* podcast: https://www.starterstory.com/stories/how-i-grinded-for-years-to-build-6m-year-bare-performance-nutrition.

The second instance where discounting is a smart play is when you're securing a high-lifetime-value customer with a breakeven sale. For example, let's say you sell a product that has frequent repeat purchasers. If your customers stick around for at least a few months, then, on average, you can afford to break even or take a slight loss on the initial sale. Over time, you'll come out way ahead.

Take Quip, the oral care brand. They're confident in their electric toothbrush product, and they know their customer lifetime value, so they include your first replacement brush for free. This gets new customers into a high-value replenishment plan quickly. Quip takes the financial loss on the initial replacement just fine because most customers continue using their product. Over the long haul, the automatic replenishment plan generates above and beyond the value needed to cover the initial loss.

Even then, it is worth noting this is an *offer* and not a dollar or percentage off *discount*.

In these two instances, discounting *isn't* putting a bucket under a leaking pipe. It's more like adding a pump to move the water through faster. But this only works when your foundations are rock solid.

"DISCOUNTS ARE A SCALPEL, NOT A SLEDGEHAMMER"

Patrick Campbell, CEO of ProfitWell, was curious about how discounting impacted key e-commerce metrics. So he did what he usually does—he pulled the data. Campbell looked at data from forty-two hundred subscription e-commerce brands and discovered a few interesting takeaways.[78]

First, it's true e-commerce brands indeed face a "trust gap" with new consumers. Trust isn't the default these days, and consumers need a compelling reason to trust a brand with their money. Discounts can incentivize consumers to hurdle over the trust gap. Or, as Campbell put it, "Discounts lower the activation energy of a lead converting." This is why some brands, like Quip, provide a breakeven offer up front.

But there's some nuance here. Campbell found higher discounts correlate with lower lifetime value. Also, higher discounts correlate with higher churn, *and* lower NPS, *and* lower word-of-mouth promotion. So even if you're effectively bringing in more customers with a steep cut, most of those customers aren't ideal—they're more likely to walk away and never mention your product to another potential customer.

---

78 Campbell shared this data in a Twitter thread: https://twitter.com/Patticus/status/1317113645701206016.

That's why even in the two instances where discounting makes sense, this tactic is more like a scalpel than a sledgehammer. It's not a tactic you can swing blindly to smash conversion rates and revenue. It's something you need to use cautiously and deliberately as a finely tuned instrument.

A SCALPEL BALANCED ON A SCALPEL

It may be most accurate to say discounting is a scalpel balanced on a scalpel. Not only must you use the tactic with extreme care, but you also need to balance *how much* you discount on a razor's edge.

Unless the average order value is in the several hundred dollars range, most consumers view anything less than 20 percent as a not-worth-it discount. Yet, if you go much higher, you start taking a big chunk out of margins and entering those low-LTV and high-churn danger zones. There's a reason commerce's most famous coupon, the Bed Bath & Beyond blue, is 20 percent. Co-founder Warren Eisenberg said, "Ten percent, we felt like it was nothing. Thirty percent we couldn't afford."[79]

---

79 Explore the history of the big blue coupon at Ron Lieber, "An Oral History of the World's Biggest Coupon," *The New York Times*, December 19, 2020, https://www.nytimes.com/2020/12/19/business/bed-bath-and-beyond-coupon.html.

One other word of caution: even though a scalpel is much smaller than a sledgehammer, it is still deadly if you don't use it correctly. (I'll leave the outcomes up to your imagination here.) The same is true for discounts. Campbell found that even *periodic* high discounts—the kind you offer only a few times a year—seem to negatively influence churn and lifetime value. As holidays expand from one-day sales to one-week or one-month sales, these perils will only increase for smaller brands.

So where does this leave e-commerce brands when it comes to incentivizing sales and attracting new-to-file customers? Are they darned if they do and darned if they don't?

In a word, no. One other intriguing discovery Campbell made is this: bundling and promotions work better than percentage discounts. Meaning there are other ways to effectively convert prospective and returning customers *without* offering a percentage off. Other research backs him up.

INNUMERACY AND WHY IT'S GOOD NEWS FOR YOUR BRAND

Most folks aren't gifted with the ability to do on-the-fly math calculations. This deficit is called innumeracy, and in a book by the same name, Professor of Mathematics John Allen Paulos defines it as "an inability to deal comfortably

with the fundamental notions of numbers and chance."[80]
Fractions, it seems, are tough for just about everyone.

This might explain why consumers perceive a 50 percent increase in quantity better than a 33 percent discount in price when they're the same economic offering.[81] Why does this happen? Researcher and Professor Ashkay Rao discovered it's because we tend to ignore the base value of products and focus instead on how big the percentage offering is.[82] That is, we think "fifty is greater than thirty-three, so 50 percent more must be a better deal than 33 percent off." Rao found this cognitive error is particularly true for less expensive and familiar products. For example, quantity increases are particularly compelling when we're purchasing things like soda, body care products, and food compared to, say, a $700 baby monitor that tracks infant sleep motions.

An implication of this and similar research is that e-commerce brands have many opportunities to get creative with their promotions. And those creative alternatives are often just as effective—or even *more* effective—at incentivizing customers without the many dangerous side effects of discounts.

---

80 John Allen Paulos, *Innumeracy: Mathematical Illiteracy and Its Consequences* (New York: Hill & Wang, 1988).

81 Haipeng (Allan) Chen, Howard Marmorstein, Michael Tsiros, and Akshay R. Rao, 2012. "When More Is Less: The Impact of Base Value Neglect on Consumer Preferences for Bonus Packs over Price Discounts," *Journal of Marketing* 76, no. 4 (2012): 64–77, jstor.org/stable/41714499?seq=1.

82 Rao explains this funky thinking at https://www.youtube.com/watch?v=qQ68iGNG1YE.

Discounts | Vs. | Promotions

THE HEALTHY ALTERNATIVES TO DISCOUNTS

Keep in mind, discounting refers to direct dollar discounts or taking a percentage off your price. Discounts encourage the consumer to look at price as the main (or only) push toward a conversion.

Promotions or offers, on the other hand, share the same goal of discounts (a conversion), but they go about it differently. Promotions offer additional value to the customers—something they wouldn't otherwise receive. With promotions, the consumer is encouraged to look at value first and price second, not the other way around.

Effective promotions include:

- Free gift with purchase
- "Buy one, get one" BOGO offers
- Free shipping and/or free returns
- Loyalty or membership perks
- Rarity (e.g., "Only 150 ever made")
- Well-timed product launches

And that's just a sampling. Many other variations effectively prompt action while highlighting product, brand, or service value.

PAIRING A LIMITED EDITION, SEASONALITY, AND REDUCED PRICE

Keep in mind, you can mix and match the alternatives I've listed. Recently, one of The Good's consumer packaged goods clients did exactly this. They launched a limited-edition product with a seasonal flavor and a reduced price. So this brand paired a reduced-cost (not a discounted) item with a genuine urgency play (limited seasonal release). It was a smart move.

The number of transactions went up 5 percent, the average number of products per transaction increased, gross revenue increased by 9 percent, and their conversion rate increased by 0.5 percent. Overall, between 10 percent and 15 percent of total revenue for the quarter came from this one limited-release product.

Similar experiments other brands could run include a bundle that includes a seasonal item at a reduced price or a "free seasonal item with purchase" once the customer hits a minimum cart value.

For a particularly mold-breaking promotion, look no further than Allbirds. For Black Friday 2020, Allbirds did something no consumer would expect—they *increased* prices. They raised the price of every item in every collection by one dollar. When a consumer made a purchase, Allbirds donated the extra dollar *and* an additional one-dollar match to youth-led climate movement Fridays for Future.[83] Plus, they released two exclusive holiday styles with a design feature highlighting the products' carbon impacts (tying into the one-dollar theme).

The move was unprecedented but on-brand for what core consumers expect, and the new styles helped generate buzz and interest.

"The more creative and the less drastic the discount promotion, the better the odds of increased brand equity in the long-term," said Web Smith, Founder of 2PM. "For many retailers, the best Black Friday deal is holding as firm as possible on pricing, service, and consumer trust."[84]

83 Cara Salpini, "Allbirds to Raise Prices on Black Friday to Fight Climate Change," Retail Dive, November 9, 2020, https://www.retaildive.com/news/allbirds-to-raise-prices-on-black-friday-to-fight-climate-change/588643/.

84 Aaron Orendorff, "Data on 400+ Ecommerce Holiday Campaigns: 2,638 Examples with Downloadable Screenshots & 10 Strategies to Guide You," Common Thread Collective (2020), https://commonthreadco.com/blogs/coachs-corner/holiday-campaigns-successful.

INVEST IN PREVENTATIVE MEASURES OVER CORRECTIVE ONES

By far the best thing you can do for your brand is invest in preventative measures more so than corrective ones. Don't default to discounts to correct leaky funnels. Instead, invest in getting outside the jar, improving the customer experience, and other conversion rate optimization fundamentals. These will all strengthen your funnel far more than applying discounts and give you the foundation you need to run more creative promotions effectively.

CHAPTER 9

LAW: YOUR COMPETITION IS A DISTRACTION

Big idea: Do you have any idea how a tactic is working out for your competitor? There is a reason racehorses wear blinders.

"Okay, now, look at where you want the car to go."

It's one of the first lessons white-knuckled parents teach their twitchy driving-permit-holding teens.

If you focus on the lane straight ahead, the car drifts down the lane. If you focus on the eighteen-wheeler on the opposite side of the road, the car drifts toward the eighteen-wheeler. We move toward the things we fixate on—it's how our brains and bodies are wired.

This is why focusing on other lanes is so dangerous. Whether they contain an eighteen-wheeler or a hefty business competitor, the more we look in their direction, the more we veer off course toward them.

THE WICKED STEPSISTERS OF E-COMMERCE

Val Geisler, Customer Evangelist at Klayvio, has called two cognitive biases, following the leader and confirmation bias, the "wicked stepsisters of e-commerce."[85]

Following the leader, or sometimes called the sunflower bias, is where we defer to authority because they're an authority. For example, see brands with big followings or big stock valuations implement a tactic and think, "Hey, we should do that, too!" These big brands stick out as the leaders of a niche or vertical, so we assume their decision is a good one, and we're quick to emulate it.

The other wicked stepsister is confirmation bias, which is where we interpret new evidence as proof of something we already believe. (This is the same bias that keeps many retailers stuck in the jar.) This bias is a stepsister because

---

85   *Finding Clarity* podcast, episode 3: https://pca.st/3dhp19ei.

as other brands follow the "we should do that, too" line of thinking, they start implementing the big competitor's approach. And so we start seeing the leader's tactic in more places. This seems to "confirm" it's a good approach and supports our theory it's worth implementing.

Together, these two biases explain how some of the most common—and most obnoxious—gimmicks have spread their way through e-commerce. For example, the bottom-right-corner pop-ups that say, "Sal from Austin, TX just bought this product." (Who cares?) Or worse, the Spin-to-Win discount roulette wheel (which makes a pop-up more disruptive and further promotes unsustainable discounting).

Although these tactics are, at best, distracting to the customer journey, the real issue actually isn't so much the tactic itself. It's how the brand got there. "The roulette wheel is not the problem. The dynamic of looking around you and desperately attempting to understand what 'works'—that is the problem. And it is maybe the single most corrosive force in e-commerce design decisions."[86]

---

86 *Finding Clarity* podcast, episode 3.

WHEN COMPETITORS ARE USEFUL AND WHEN THEY'RE NOT

"Sure," you might say, "but it's still important to know *where* that eighteen-wheeler is on the road."

I agree.

To revisit the driving example, you certainly want to know there's an eighteen-wheeler in the other lane, even as you focus on your own. That general awareness is healthy and informs your steering. It's when awareness becomes a fixation that you're heading toward danger.

Likewise, there are both healthy and unhealthy ways to be aware of the competition.

Healthy vs. Un-Healthy ways to Look at Competition

HEALTHY WAYS OF LOOKING AT COMPETITORS

Some of the healthy ways to study your competitors include indirect audience research and identifying testing ideas.

Indirect audience research is when you observe your audience online instead of directly engaging with them—for example, through one-on-one customer interviews. Several effective forms of indirect customer research involve checking out your competitors. For example, social listening. This is where you round up comments that potential customers have made about competitors on Twitter, Instagram, or other platforms. Then you analyze sentiments, common themes, and other trends in their commentary.

This can be a useful way to start collecting voice-of-customer (the words and phrases customers use) to inform your campaigns and messaging. Doing so can give you a roundabout idea of what's important to customers when they buy a product, where they're dissatisfied with the competitor, and other contextual clues such as what prompted a purchase. These qualitative clues can all help you identify tests to run on your site.

For example, let's say you sell cookware, and a direct competitor's nonstick piece scratches easily. Customers mention this often in their social media complaints, often paired with the rage emoji. Based on this clue, you may hypothesize highlighting your product's durability in ads or on the product detail page may improve conversions.

Essentially, what you're doing in this example is looking

for important or prominent insights in qualitative data and using those findings to inform tests.

Importance is where you uncover a problem or factor that may not be relevant to one segment of potential customers but is very important to a small key segment. The pain isn't widespread, but it's acute for a specific group. To stick with the cookware example, this may be a small segment of customers who complain about handle discoloration and extreme heat transfer on gas stovetops.

Prominence often involves the opposite—the pain isn't acute, but it's widespread. Many potential customers experience and cite it. For example, the "red" Dutch oven is more reddish-orange than true red.

Identifying either of these in market or audience research can help you brainstorm solutions to test on your site.

What makes this approach healthy is your posture toward the competitor. You're like Kobe Bryant studying tapes of your basketball heroes, identifying what was effective or ineffective (based on traceable outcomes), and adapting their moves to the unique skills you have as a player.

You're looking at how things are going for others and asking questions such as "Why was that effective in the context of the overall game?" and "Does it fit with who I am and what I'm doing?"

This is a very different approach than blind copying.

UNHEALTHY WAYS OF LOOKING AT COMPETITORS

In contrast, unhealthy ways of looking at the competition almost always involves directly lifting something—messaging, strategy, tactics, and so forth. It involves blind copying.

Your posture here isn't observation, learning, or testing. It's far more pernicious—it's banking on a shortcut. It's assuming what works for them will work for you (without adaptation to your audience or brand!) and is therefore worth plagiarizing.

This is not only risky; it's a poor approach to building a profitable e-commerce business.

POACHING VERSUS PROVEN APPROACHES

Before I go deep into the risks of copying, it's important you understand what I'm not saying: I'm not saying you neglect proven approaches.

For example, some of the most successful e-commerce brands

out there send phenomenal welcome emails. You should, too, not because it's what the competitor does but because data and experience prove this is a highly effective way to build relationships with new customers.

Likewise for displaying clear shipping prices, researching your customers, providing excellent support, and many other tried-and-true methods of delighting customers and building brand equity. These are all foundational approaches supported by data across industries. They're good things to implement for any e-commerce brand.

There's a stark difference between adapting a proven tactic for your brand and copying an unproven one from a competitor.

WHY FIXATING ON COMPETITORS IS ALWAYS A BAD IDEA

Some of the best racehorses of all time (see Secretariat) trained with blinders. Because of where horses' eyes are and how they're structured, horses can see nearly everything around them. They also process motion in their field of vision very quickly. These facts mean racehorses, especially younger ones, are easily spooked and distracted from their race goals.

To prevent distractions, trainers equip the horse with blinders, or blinkers, that limit the horse's field of vision to the track.

Excellent peripheral vision, it seems, isn't a strength when you're trying to focus on a goal. This is true for e-commerce leaders as well for a handful of reasons.

YOUR AUDIENCE IS NOT THE SAME AS THEIR AUDIENCE

I've had footwear brands say to me, "Oh, but Nike is doing this, so we need to do it, too." This is a prime example of one of the wicked stepsisters (follow the leader and confirmation bias) in action.

The logic is, "we're a newer shoe company, and they've been a shoe company for decades, so we need to follow their lead." This reasoning misses all the nuance of context. For starters, Nike's market cap is in the billions, and they have LeBron James and a whole host of other all-star athletes on their team. Their name recognition far outpaces newer shoe brands.

Plus, there's no guarantee whatever move Nike just made targets the same customers of the footwear brand sitting in front of me. Simply operating in the same vertical (e.g., running shoes) doesn't ensure you target the same customer segment. The runners who buy Nike racing shoe releases regardless of PR headlines are likely a very different segment from the runners who buy Allbirds's Tree Dasher running shoe for sustainability values.

This isn't just true for running shoes either. You see clear segment differences in almost every competitive e-commerce landscape: mattresses, nonalcoholic drinks, cookware, and eyeglasses, to name a few. Remember the example of the three eyeglass brands The Good has worked with? One catered to heavy computer users, another to older adults and stylish readers, and the third to sports enthusiasts. They were all three "glasses companies," but they had different audiences, advertising strategies, and seasonality. They weren't apples to apples.

YOUR BIGGEST COMPETITOR MAY NOT BE YOUR BIGGEST COMPETITOR

A closely related danger of focusing on your biggest competitors is, well, they may not even be your biggest competitors.

It's easy to assume brands with similar products are your biggest threat. But this really depends on your target audience and positioning. If you're a nonalcoholic DTC drink startup, you may assume your biggest threat is another nonalcoholic DTC business. That could be true. Or your biggest threat might be the seltzer water with a splash of lemon the prospect can make at home. Or the kombucha on sale at Whole Foods. Netflix, for example, competes with "all the activities that consumers have at their disposal in their leisure time...reading a book, surfing YouTube...going out to dinner with friends or enjoying a glass of wine."[87]

The point is, it's tough to know who your true competitors are unless you're actively talking with your customers and digging into their journey toward you.

YOU WEREN'T IN THE ROOM WHERE IT HAPPENED

Lin-Manuel Miranda's hit Broadway play *Hamilton* has plenty of catchy songs. One of them is called "The Room Where It Happens," and a section of it goes like this: "No one really knows how the parties get to 'Yes' / The pieces that are sacrificed in every game of chess / We just assume that it happens / But no one else is in the room where it happens."

The song refers to a secret deal that affects America's future, but it pretty much sums up how well you understand your competitor's tactics, too.

Without being in the room where they made the decision, you've little context for it. You don't know if the idea was inspired by liquor or guessing, the founders' five-year-old,

---

87   Netflix's responses to top investor questions: https://ir.netflix.net/ir-overview/top-investor-questions/default.aspx.

or hard-backed data. You don't know if what you're seeing on their home page is a test (perhaps you're in a test group), an untested assumption, a move to copy one of *their* competitors, or the winning variant of a carefully calculated A/B experiment.

What's more, you've no idea how that decision is playing out. It could be tanking home page conversion rates and they haven't caught it yet. It could be driving away a very valuable customer segment (maybe to you!). Or it could be working beautifully.

You just don't know. You weren't in the room where it happened. And so, if you copy their moves, you've no idea whether you're cheating off a valedictorian or a flunky.

SIMPLY PUT, COPYING IS NOT HOW GREAT STRATEGY WORKS

Great strategy (whether it's marketing, conversion rate optimization, or sales) depends on great inputs. "Garbage in, garbage out," as they say.

Keep in mind, "garbage" here is very contextual. A half pound of vine-ripe tomatoes is a great ingredient if you're making margherita pizza but a garbage ingredient if you're making a strawberry banana smoothie.

Likewise with strategy. Your brand isn't in a bubble. It's in the context of all the other ingredients (audience, team strengths, economy, etc.) working toward a specific recipe (your business goals). Whatever you're copying from competitors may not be a garbage input for them. But there's a strong probability it's a garbage input for you because *you're making something different.*

If you *do* wind up using similar ingredients or techniques, it should be because it's what's best for your business and strategy, not because it's what a competitor is doing.

ON FOMO AND SHORT-LIVED CHANNEL TRENDS

Keep in mind, trends can lose efficacy as quickly as they gain it. This is especially true with marketing channels.

In 2016, the engagement rate for sponsored Instagram posts hovered around 4 percent. By 2019, these rates had slid to 1.9 percent. Nonsponsored posts saw a similar dip.[88] The number of organic Google searches that receive a click and the reach of Facebook posts have likewise fluctuated a concerning amount.

88 Robert Williams, "Instagram Influencer Engagement Hovers Near All-Time Lows, Study Says," Marketing Dive, July 9, 2019, https://www.marketingdive.com/news/instagram-influencer-engagement-hovers-near-all-time-lows-study-says/558331/.

Channels change. They become more effective or less effective depending on usage and saturation. Things that don't lose efficacy, on the other hand, are understanding your customers, their experience, and why they buy from you.

Take RH, formerly known as Restoration Hardware. You won't find the brand posting on social media, and that's intentional. CEO Gary Friedman explains their focus is on producing work that's so good that their customers talk on their behalf. "We don't have Instagram, yet we are the most-Instagrammed brand in our industry," says Friedman. "We don't have Pinterest, but we are the most-pinned home brand." This seems to work just fine for RH, too. In 2012, RH's annual revenue was $958 million. Seven years later, it reported $2.6 billion. All without social media.

YOUR TIME AND ENERGY ARE FINITE—HOW WILL YOU USE THEM?

No matter who you are or what brand you're running, your time and energy are finite.

Even with the most effective health hacks out there, there are only so many tasks you can tackle each day. Why spend your limited resources on monitoring and worrying over the other team? Worry, it's been said, is a waste of creativity. And there are far better—far higher ROI—ways you can spend your creativity, time, and energy than worrying over whatever your competitor is doing.

UNDERSTAND YOUR SPECIFIC CUSTOMERS' DATA

The best way is, by far, understanding your specific consumers' data. Start gathering all the information you can that's related to whatever challenge you're facing. Look at the quantitative and qualitative data, the customer experience, leaks in the funnel, and anything else. Use all that information (not what competitors are doing) to contextually diagnose and start treating a problem.

LOOK FOR COMPARATIVE EXPERIENCES, NOT JUST COMPETITIVE ONES

If you're stuck on how to treat the problem, another high-ROI activity is casting a wide inspiration net beyond your competitors. Web Smith of 2PM notes, "If more DTC execs studied adjacent industries, I believe they'd find more arbitrage opportunities for growth and sustainability. There would also be fewer category competitors, i.e., ten [DTC xyz] launches in six months. Less outsourcing strategy, more studying of the machine."[89] (He also tellingly says

---

89 Web made this comment on Twitter: https://twitter.com/web/status/1193687868625043464.

if he had to do it all over again, he would've ignored competitors in the earliest stages of building a DTC brand.)[90]

At The Good, this means the team doesn't just look at competitive experiences; they look at comparative ones, too. They draw ideas from totally left-field industries that face comparable solutions or offer comparative experiences. For example, if we're trying to figure out how to help customers select a paint chip, we may look at how customers choose fabrics, rugs, or even clothing. Then we take any creative ideas we find and ask whether they're worth testing in the paint brand's context.

COMPETE WITH YOURSELF FIRST AND FOREMOST

A third good use of your time and energy is competing with yourself. Competition *does* have many benefits. The stress of competing (up to a certain level) can heighten your creativity and focus. Plus, winning a competition can release dopamine—that feel-good chemical messenger—further fueling your motivation. It feels good to win, so we like to keep winning.

The trick is, you want to use these benefits of competing to take your brand to new heights, not across lanes toward a competitor. To stay in your lane, look at your own rates

---

90 Web made this comment on Twitter: https://twitter.com/web/status/1188848477108703234.

and data and ask, "How can we make this incrementally better?" Remember, a good conversion rate is one that's always improving, not one that's mimicking another brand or a loosely established industry baseline.

CONCLUSION

Optimizing your site for conversions isn't simple. To do it well, you'll need to customize the experience for your specific site's visitors. This means there's no one-size-fits-all template I can hand you. But the path to success **does** have patterns. And if you follow those proven patterns and the underlying principles, I promise you'll find success.

The good news is that in reading this book, you now know the patterns for success. I've swum through the choppy waters, learned all the lessons, and taken careful note of the recurring trends before documenting them within these pages.

You have the recipe. Now you just need to put the ingredients to work.

By taking action today, you'll be ahead of the estimated 91.2 percent of the top one million websites who are ***not optimizing*** with A/B testing software for an improved user experience.[91]

Optimize with testing, and you'll be in the top 8.8 percent of website experiences.

I don't know about you, but I like those odds and what it means for your customers and revenue.

WHAT NEXT?

Growing conversions online is an art and a science, and it takes constant effort to achieve strong results. The Good is here to help if you are stuck or need help in improving your site's conversion rates.

If you are managing the process yourself, be sure to check out https://thegood.com/insights for resources to help you along the way. You'll find detailed, tactical advice that will help you apply the principles in this book. (You can also find plenty of tactical advice in my previous book, *Stop Marketing, Stop Selling*, at https://thegood.com/book or on Amazon.)

---

91 According to BuiltWith's analysis of A/B testing usage distribution in the top one million sites: https://trends.builtwith.com/analytics/a-b-testing.

If you need help and want to increase online conversions dramatically, visit https://thegood.com/services to learn how The Good can put our experience to work for your brand.

If you want to have me speak at your next event, interview me for your podcast, or just say hello, you can reach me at https://jonmacdonald.com.

Thanks for reading. Here's to a better internet for everyone.

9 781544 524962